10-MINUTE
DIGITAL
DECLUTTER

THE SIMPLE HABIT TO ELIMINATE TECHNOLOGY OVERLOAD

By: Barrie Davenport
LiveBoldAndBloom.com

and

S.J. Scott
www.HabitBooks.com

Publishing services provided by  **Archangel Ink**

ISBN: 1519555652
ISBN-13: 978-1519555656

DISCLAIMER

No part of this publication may be reproduced or transmitted in any form or by any means, mechanical or electronic, including photocopying or recording, or by any information storage and retrieval system, or transmitted by email without permission in writing from the publisher.

While all attempts have been made to verify the information provided in this publication, neither the author nor the publisher assumes any responsibility for errors, omissions, or contrary interpretations of the subject matter herein.

This book is for entertainment purposes only. The views expressed are those of the author alone, and should not be taken as expert instruction or commands. The reader is responsible for his or her own actions.

Adherence to all applicable laws and regulations, including international, federal, state, and local governing professional licensing, business practices, advertising, and all other aspects of doing business in the United States, Canada, or any other jurisdiction is the sole responsibility of the purchaser or reader.

Neither the author nor the publisher assumes any responsibility or liability whatsoever on the behalf of the purchaser or reader of these materials.

Any perceived slight of any individual or organization is purely unintentional.

YOUR FREE GIFT

As a way of saying *thanks* for your purchase, I'm offering a free report that's exclusive to my book and blog readers.

In *77 Good Habits to Live a Better Life*, you'll discover a variety of routines that can help you in many different areas of your life. You will learn how to make lasting changes to your work, success, learning, health, and sleep habits.

Go Here to Grab 77 Good Habits to Live a Better Life:
www.developgoodhabits.com/free

YOUR FREE GIFT (2)

As a way of saying thank you for your purchase, I hope you'll enjoy **39 Power Habits of Wildly Successful People**.

These are daily and weekly habits to improve your health, relationships, personal growth, and career success. Prioritize the habits most important to you, and begin working on them one by one. I hope you enjoy this free book.

LiveBoldandBloom.com/39-habits

TABLE OF CONTENTS

Part I: Introduction...1

   The Dangers of Digital Clutter and Technology Overwhelm ...3

Part II: The Importance Of Digital Decluttering...............11

   Why You Feel Overwhelmed by Technology 13

   Why We Get Hooked on Technology 15

   How Digital Dependence Damages Your Life 19

   How to Identify Your Life Priorities
   (beyond the Digital World)..23

   The Benefit of the Digital Decluttering Habit......................27

   14 Advantages of a Digital Decluttered Life 31

Part III: Getting Started With Digital Decluttering...........37

   6 Types of Digital Clutter 39

   Do You Have a Decluttering Problem? (21 Questions to Ask
   Yourself) 43

   8 Steps to the 10-Minute Digital Declutter Habit 47

   8 Actions for Starting Your First Decluttering Project...........53

   7 Questions to Ask While Decluttering 57

Part IV: Decluttering Your Social Media Activities............**59**

17 Strategies to Minimize Your Social Media Activities..........61

Part V: Decluttering Your Email Inbox............................**69**

8 Steps to Organize Your Email Inbox 71

Part VI: Decluttering Your Computer **79**

The Truth about the Clutter on Your Computer....................81

How to Create a Simple File System.......................................83

6 Ways to Organize Your Folders and Files 89

7 Steps for Creating a Minimalist Computer..........................95

Part VII: Decluttering Your Smartphone And Tablet.........**99**

Smartphones: The Positives and the Negatives 101

How to Declutter Your Smartphone (9 Action Steps)...........103

8 Quality Apps to Add to Your Smartphone..........................109

Part VIII: Protecting Your Digital Life **115**

The Importance of Protecting Your Digital Life...................117

Use "The Rule of Three" for Your Digital Backups.............119

6 Simple Steps to Backing up Your Digital Life 121

4 Concerns about Cloud-Based Backups 127

The Importance of Creating Solid Passwords........................131

Part IX: Maintaining Your Digital Declutter Action Plan 135

The Quarterly Digital Decluttering Habit 137

Conclusion: Get Started with Your Digital Manifesto 145

Did You Like 10-Minute Digital Declutter? 149

More Books by Barrie 151

More Books by Steve 153

About the Authors 155

PART I

INTRODUCTION

THE DANGERS OF DIGITAL CLUTTER AND TECHNOLOGY OVERWHELM

Once upon a time, families sat down at a table for dinner in the evening and talked about their day as they ate.

After dinner, children did homework using a pencil and paper, often looking up facts in a collection of hardbound books called "encyclopedias." Meanwhile, Mom and Dad would read a printed newspaper or gather around the radio to listen to the news or a comedy show. Sometimes the family would play a game, take a walk, or simply share a fun activity together.

If they needed to communicate with someone outside the home, they would write a letter, meet somewhere, or make a phone call from the *single* household phone.

No one was texting, sexting, emailing, surfing, gaming, downloading, bookmarking, blogging, or podcasting. They weren't watching TV, streaming video, or hopping from one YouTube video to the next. There was no Facebook, Twitter, Instagram, Snapchat, Pinterest, or LinkedIn. In fact, the only form of instant communication was shouting to others in the next room.

In the last twenty-five years, we have drastically changed how we socialize, spend our time, do our work, and entertain ourselves. According to the Pew Research Center[1], today, eight in ten US adults

---

[1] http://www.pewinternet.org/2014/02/27/part-1-how-the-internet-has-woven-itself-into-american-life/

(81 percent) say they use laptop and desktop computers at home, work, school, and everywhere in between. Meanwhile, 90 percent of US adults have a cell phone, and two-thirds of those adults use their phones to go online.

In a relatively short amount of time, the Internet has shifted from an occasional tool to the primary way we work, communicate, and entertain ourselves. Recent research reveals that **the average time spent per week on email, text, and social media is about 23 hours**.

Although the amount of time spent online continues to grow, **62 percent of the respondents to the research survey stated they want to _decrease_ the amount of time spent online in favor of more face-to-face interactions**. Unfortunately, their actions contradict their desire to disconnect.

It appears we're obsessed with technology, and it's impacting every aspect of how we live our lives. We have become such slaves to the gadgets that were _supposed_ to simplify our lives. These days, we prefer the quick fix of instant information and low-quality entertainment over real-world interactions and experiences.

Just pull back the curtain on the new dinnertime ritual and you will see that every member of the family is engrossed in their smartphone or tablet, checking email, texting, or playing a game in between forkfuls of food.

Teenagers would rather chat by text or Snapchat than meet up in person. They're too busy taking "selfies" to coordinate togetherness. Children can look up any homework question online and get the answer in seconds without using much brain power. After dinner, family members often go to their separate rooms to spend time with their preferred electronic devices.

Nowadays, we keep digital devices by our beds, take them to the bathroom, and have them within finger's reach throughout the day.

According to "Moore's Law" (named after Gordon E. Moore, the co-founder of Intel), the number of transistors per square inch on integrated circuits doubled every year since the integrated circuit was invented, and he predicted this trend would continue for the foreseeable future. The pace slowed down a bit in later years, but data density has doubled approximately every eighteen months, which is the current definition of Moore's Law.

That said, it's important to recognize that technology has given countless advantages to our modern lives.

Both Steve and Barrie (the authors of this book) rely heavily on digital technology to run their online businesses. They owe most of their lifestyle freedom to the opportunities that come from computers and similar devices.

However, they also recognize the need for balance in their lives. Digital devices are convenient, but they can also have negative effects on your time and energy.

From inboxes congested with years' worth of emails to thousands of unused computer files, your digital clutter can grow like untended weeds in a garden. These items can have a similar negative impact on your life, similar to physical clutter in your home. When you're buried under hundreds of old files, you'll often experience feelings of overwhelm, anxiety, and confusion.

Digital "stuff" also has an insidious way of occupying your time with nonessential activities that don't make you feel any happier.

The more time you spend surfing the Net, hanging out on social media, or playing a mobile app game, the less time you have to hang out with your friends, enjoy nature, or simply get more out of life.

A digital-world addiction can be as destructive as other types of addictions. Compulsive use of technology interferes with your daily life, work, and relationships in a number of ways. When you spend more time with your online friends than your real ones, or you can't stop yourself from compulsively checking your email or social media, you're allowing these devices to control you instead of the other way around.

While it's true that the information age is here to stay, there is a solution to finding that balance between using digital technology to your advantage and living life to the fullest.

The solution will be detailed in the following book, *10-Minute Digital Declutter: The Simple Habit to Eliminate Technology Overload.*

About 10-Minute Declutter

This book is for anyone who feels overwhelmed by the emails, media, documents, photos, videos, and apps that consume their daily life. It's written for the person who is starting to recognize the danger of "digital noise," but doesn't know how to live in this modern world without experiencing the feeling of overwhelm.

It's also for those who need a system for the information they *do* want. Not only will you get back more time, you'll also discover core strategies for maximizing the time you spend in the digital world.

This book will be a good fit if you

- Feel overwhelmed by the sheer volume of information on your devices
- Can't easily find the emails, documents, or websites you're looking for
- Have little time to tackle a big digital declutter and organizing project
- Feel embarrassed and drained by the clutter and disorganization
- Find yourself afraid to delete anything for fear you might need it one day
- Feel yourself giving away too much time and energy to the virtual world
- Would like to change your priorities and learn to step away from your devices more often
- Get complaints from your boss, spouse, or family members about your digital clutter or disorganization, or about the time you spend online
- Simply desire a more organized, minimalist lifestyle

The bottom line?

If you have a desire to live an organized, simplified digital life—and to reclaim some of the time you spend with digital devices—then you're reading the right book. Throughout *10-Minute Digital Declutter*, you will learn both the strategies to organize your devices and how to make them part of a daily habit.

Who Are We?

Barrie is the founder of an award-winning personal development site, Live Bold and Bloom. She is a certified personal coach and online-course creator, helping people apply practical, evidence-based solutions and strategies to push past comfort zones and create happier, richer, more successful lives. She is also the author of a series of self-improvement books on positive habits, life passion, confidence building, mindfulness, and simplicity.

As an entrepreneur, a mom of three, and a homeowner, Barrie knows firsthand how valuable and life-changing it is to simplify, prioritize, and organize your physical *and* digital life.

Steve (or "S.J.") runs the blog Develop Good Habits, and is the author of a series of habit-related titles, all of which are available at HabitBooks.com. The goal of his content is to show how continuous habit development can lead to a better life.

The main reason Steve felt inspired to write this book is that he is expecting his first child in March 2016. Like any father-to-be, he worries about the world his son will live in. Specifically, he sees the danger of being too reliant on technology pervasive throughout society. His hope is to raise his children to leverage the digital world, but not allow it to dominate their lives.

Together, we are the authors of the companion piece to this book called *10-Minute Declutter: The Stress-Free Habit for Simplifying Your Home.*

While we covered many strategies for simplification in our previous book, we barely touched on the subject of digital clutter. So this book is a follow-up where we show you how to organize your technology.

As you can see, the following book is a collaborative effort between Steve and Barrie. We both provide information and knowledge from research, outside experts, and our personal experiences.

For instance, while writing this book, Barrie moved from Atlanta, Georgia, to Asheville, North Carolina, and went through the process of decluttering and downsizing her possessions to live in a much smaller home. After completing the move, Barrie decided to tackle the one project she's avoided since becoming an online entrepreneur—decluttering and organizing her technology.

After implementing the strategies we outline in *10-Minute Digital Declutter*, Barrie has now embraced the idea that it's equally important to keep her virtual world organized as it is to maintain a tidy, organized home.

On the other hand, Steve comes to this book with a different perspective. Like many productivity enthusiasts, he's always looking for shortcuts to save time.

What attracted him to the concept of digital decluttering is the idea that any time saved with technology is more time he'll have to live life. So, in the past few months, he has made the conscious decision to identify the technology that's truly important, and how he can proactively ignore everything else.

As you can see, we each have different experiences when it comes to minimizing our digital lives. By reading the following book, you will discover a wealth of actionable advice that can assist *your* efforts at digital decluttering.

Three "Housekeeping Items" to Keep in Mind

Just like we did in *10-Minute Declutter*, we want you to keep three things in mind as you read this book.

First, you probably noticed that we use the third-person tense (e.g., "Steve remembers . . ." or "Barrie suggests . . .") when sharing anecdotes about our experiences. This was done specifically to make it easier for you to follow the narrative of the book. We admit it's a bit clunky, but you will find it's easier to grasp the information if you know who is telling the story.

Secondly, as mentioned earlier, digital technology evolves at an exponential rate. It seems like as soon as an application is released, it quickly becomes outdated or replaced by a superior product. For that reason, we will often stick to more generalized suggestions for managing your online information, and *only* offer specific suggestions for a tool if we believe it will be around for a long time.

Finally, if you're married or live with a partner, then you should share this book with them. Perhaps you can work together to knock out these 10-minute decluttering projects.

If you have children who use digital devices, you can assign them short decluttering tasks that are easy and fun. This will teach them the importance of personal responsibility and how to manage their own digital worlds. This is also a great time to teach your kids the value of disengaging from devices and spending more time in real-world activities and relationships.

We have a lot of ground to cover, so let's jump in and discuss why we are so devoted to our devices, and how that is impacting us.

PART II

THE IMPORTANCE OF DIGITAL DECLUTTERING

WHY YOU FEEL OVERWHELMED BY TECHNOLOGY

> *"The constant dilemma of the information age is that our ability to gather a sea of data greatly exceeds the tools and techniques available to sort, extract, and apply the information we've collected."*
>
> - Jeff Davidson, work-life balance expert, author, columnist

We've all experienced that feeling of overwhelm when it comes to the digital world. According to Dr. Daniel Levitin, McGill University psychology professor and author of *The Organized Mind: Thinking Straight in the Age of Information Overload*[2], human beings have created more information in the last ten years than in all recorded history prior.

Dr. Martin Hilbert and his team at the University of Southern California conducted a study[3], published in the journal *Science,* to calculate the world's total technological capacity—how much information humankind is able to store, communicate, and compute. What he found was startling. With the growth of the Internet, 24-hour television, and mobile phones, we now receive five times as much information every day as we did in 1986.

---

[2] http://www.amazon.com/The-Organized-Mind-Thinking-Information/dp/052595418X

[3] http://www.sciencemag.org/content/332/6025/60.abstract

However, this statistic pales in comparison to the growth of information we generate through email, social media, and text messages. Studies have shown that the average social media user consumes 285 pieces of content a day, which equates to about 54,000 words (the length of an average novel). We encounter one thousand clickable links and are bombarded by 174 newspapers' worth of data a day just through social media alone.

If it sounds impossible to read a full book each day, keep in mind that most people now *skim* information instead of reading everything. The reason why? We simply have too much to consume on a daily basis.

With billions of people worldwide producing and consuming information, Dr. Hilbert and his researchers found that there are now 295 exabytes of data floating around the world—that's 29,500,000,000,000,000,000,000 pieces of information. This equates to 315 times the number of grains of sand on Earth.

The ability to process all this information has doubled every eighteen months with computers, and has doubled every two years with telecommunication devices. According to Dr. Hilbert's study, "In 2007, all the general-purpose computers worldwide computed 6.4×10^{18} instructions per second. This is in the same general order of magnitude as the number of nerve impulses executed by the human brain in a single second."

It appears there's no end to this exponential increase in information.

As relevant, interesting, or important as the information might be for you or your work, it's becoming increasingly urgent to create systems that allow you to sort the wheat from the chaff in the immediacy of the moment—before you are suffocated under a mountain of documents, blog posts, tweets, and text messages.

The question is: "Why have we become so reliant on this technology?" We'll answer that in the next section.

WHY WE GET HOOKED ON TECHNOLOGY

Most people *love* technology. It makes our lives easier, faster, and more expansive. But there is a diminishing point of return associated with our devotion to digital devices, and that point appears when we can't separate ourselves from them.

According to a Time Mobility poll[4], 84 percent of people worldwide said they couldn't go a single day without their mobile devices. One in four people check their phone every 30 minutes, while one in five check it every ten. Of adults aged twenty-five to thirty, 75 percent said they took their phones to bed.

It's not just adults who are hooked. Children are plenty distracted as well. According to a Kaiser Family Foundation study[5], young people ages eight to eighteen now spend nearly every waking moment when they are not in school using media—more than 7.5 hours a day.

In an interview[6] with Arianna Huffington, Richard Davidson, a professor of psychology and psychiatry at the University of Wisconsin-Madison, says, "I think if we're all honest about it, we all suffer from attention deficit disorder, and it's in part attributable to the kind of exposure we have to digital devices. The kind of feedback that we get from them is immediate feedback and it's highly reinforcing, so it

---

[4] http://techland.time.com/2012/08/16/your-life-is-fully-mobile

[5] http://kff.org/other/event/generation-m2-media-in-the-lives-of

[6] http://www.huffingtonpost.com/2014/10/03/neuroscientist-richard-da_n_5923648.html

becomes like a drug. And in fact, it co-opts the same brain systems that are indicated in addiction."

The question here is, is it *really* possible to be addicted to the digital world? The psychiatric community is beginning to think so.

In the 2013 edition of the *Diagnostic and Statistical Manual of Mental Disorders*, psychiatrists have decided to list Internet Use Disorder (IUD) as a condition "recommended for further study." That means they haven't decided yet whether IUD is a legitimate diagnosis requiring treatment, but might do so in the future.

(Source: American Psychiatric Association (2013). *Diagnostic and Statistical Manual of Mental Disorders* (Fifth ed.). Arlington, VA: American Psychiatric Publishing. pp. 797–798.)

According to the definition determined by the American Psychiatric Association, IUD is an addiction to Internet gaming with an array of symptoms including a preoccupation with gaming, withdrawal symptoms, loss of other interests and hobbies, and deception of family and friends about the extent of use.

Internet Use Disorder is generally associated with online gaming, **but you don't have to be addicted to gaming to fall into the spectrum of problematic or compulsive use of digital devices**. Many scientific studies expand the definition to include excessive, obsessive online use. Any virtual activities that interfere with normal life will fit the bill, including social networking, texting, blogging, email, excessive or inappropriate Internet pornography use, or Internet shopping.

A 2014 study[7] published in the journal *Cyberpsychology, Behavior, and Social Networking* suggests that the pervasiveness of Internet addiction differs markedly among countries and is inversely related to quality of life.

Internet addiction is considered a national health crisis in China. According to an army psychologist[8] who runs a rehabilitation center in Beijing for Internet addicts, an estimated 14 percent of China's youth

---

[7] http://online.liebertpub.com/doi/abs/10.1089/cyber.2014.0317?journalCode=cyber

[8] http://www.telegraph.co.uk/news/worldnews/asia/china/11386325/Chinese-teen-chops-hand-off-to-cure-internet-addiction.html

are hooked on the Internet. It's the first country in the world to classify this diagnosis as an addiction. This addiction is the subject of a new documentary called Web Junkie[9], which follows the treatment of three Chinese teenagers who so prefer the virtual world over the real one that their lives are severely compromised.

In a 2011 study[10], Chinese researchers studied eighteen young people who were addicted to the Internet and found reductions in their brain volume compared with the brain volumes of non-addicts. The diminished brain regions of the Internet addicts included areas thought to play a role in emotional processing, executive thinking skills, attention, and cognitive control.

Some people have suggested that the "theory of variable rewards" explains our obsession with the digital world. This theory, created by American psychologist and behaviorist B.F. Skinner in the 1950s, resulted from his study of lab mice that responded more aggressively to random rewards than predictable ones. When mice pressed a lever, they sometimes got a small treat, other times a large treat, and other times nothing at all. Unlike mice that received the same treat with each lever press, the mice that received variable rewards pressed the lever more often and compulsively.

In the same way the mice compulsively press the lever, we constantly check our emails, phones, and social media because the dopamine trigger in our brains compels us to do so. Like the mice, we sometimes get a small reward, sometimes a big one, and sometimes there is a spammy ad for Viagra. But one outcome is predictable for anyone who compulsively uses digital machines—we inevitably compromise our lives, our relationships, and often our health in that search for our next "fix."

While you might not feel that technology negatively impacts your life, there have been numerous studies that prove otherwise. In the next section, we go over this research and how it demonstrates the dangers of being overly reliant on technology.

---

[9] webjunkiemovie.com

[10] http://journals.plos.org/plosone/article?id=10.1371/journal.pone.0020708

How Digital Dependence Damages Your Life

S till not convinced about the dangers of the digital world?
Sure, you might spend less time with family and friends. Maybe you aren't quite as resourceful or creative. But don't the positive qualities of technology outweigh the negatives?

Of course, there are undeniable benefits to the digital world, but for those who spend hours each day connected, there are also major negative outcomes that can severely impact the quality of your life.

Researchers[11] at the University of Gothenburg in Sweden studied the habits of more than 4,100 men and women, aged between twenty and twenty-four, and over the course of a year found that those who constantly use a computer or their mobile phone can develop stress, sleeping disorders, and depression.

Says lead author of the study, Sara Thomee, "It was easy to spend more time than planned at the computer (e.g., working, gaming, or chatting), and this tended to lead to time pressure, neglect of other activities and personal needs (such as social interaction, sleep, physical activity), as well as bad ergonomics, and mental overload."

The study also found a correlation between stress and always being available on the phone, especially relating to feelings of guilt for not replying to messages. Using the computer late at night—and losing sleep as a result—was also a risk factor for stress and reduced performance.

---

[11] http://www.gu.se/digitalAssets/1383/1383803_gupea_2077_28245_1.pdf

Other large-scale studies[12] have reinforced the link between excessive computer use and depression. Working alone on a computer can lead to a sense of isolation as workers spend less and less time interacting with other people.

There are other health dangers to overuse of digital devices, including eye strain, back and neck muscle tension, carpal tunnel syndrome, obesity (from less exercise), and sleep disorders. Sitting for too many hours a day is linked to heart disease, diabetes, and premature death.

Dr. David Greenfield, the director of the Center for Internet and Technology Addiction, suggests 90 percent of Americans fall into the category of overusing, abusing, or misusing their smartphones, according to a recent survey he did in conjunction with AT&T. His research found that 98 percent of respondents said that texting while driving is dangerous, but nearly 75 percent admit having done it. The National Safety Council reports that cell phone use while driving leads to 1.6 million crashes each year. In fact, one out of every four car accidents in the United States is caused by texting and driving.

Our reliance on technology and obsession with being constantly connected is clearly harming our relationships[13].

For instance, it was a wake-up call for Barrie the day her teenage daughter walked into her office and said, "You tell me I shouldn't spend so much time on the computer, but you're always on it now." Barrie realized she wasn't being a good role model, nor was she making it easy to have spontaneous, quality conversations with her daughter.

Not only do our virtual distractions pull us away from real-world interactions, but they also compel us to interact in disengaged and thoughtless ways through text or email. Too many people choose an impersonal email or text to break off a relationship, share bad news, or conduct arguments. The loss of real-world interactions makes it much easier to shoot off a thoughtless or hurtful text or email without the filter of looking someone in the eye.

---

[12] http://www.dailymail.co.uk/health/article-153281/Why-using-cause-depression.html

[13] http://liveboldandbloom.com/10/relationships/how-smartphones-could-be-ruining-your-relationship

Says Alex Lickman, MD, in an article for *Psychology Today*[14], "People are often uncomfortable with face-to-face confrontation, so it's easy to understand why they'd choose to use the Internet. Precisely because electronic media transmit emotion so poorly compared to in-person interaction, many view it as the perfect way to send difficult messages: It blocks us from registering the negative emotional responses such messages engender, which provides us the illusion we're not really doing harm."

When obsessive computer use interferes with your relationships, finances, or health—and you continue the excessive use despite efforts to control your behavior—then it's a serious problem.

Hopefully you aren't at the point where your computer and smartphone have become an obsession that's harmed your health or ruined a relationship. But you might relate to the temptation to jump down the rabbit hole of endless information and entertainment.

When the real world gets boring or stressful, that alluring virtual reality always awaits, tempting you to log in and tune out.

One way to loosen the grip of online overload and obsession is by creating the daily habit of decluttering your devices. We're here to help you do just that, and, as you'll learn, decluttering has a surprising effect on your time and energy. In the next section, we'll talk about the importance of identifying what you truly want and how this relates to the technology you regularly use.

---

[14] https://www.psychologytoday.com/blog/happiness-in-world/201006/the-effect-technology-relationships

How to Identify Your Life Priorities (beyond the Digital World)

We'd like to make a bold assumption here.

You probably have a secret desire to create boundaries around the excess digital clutter in your life. If you feel exhausted by the constant information overload and long to better manage the time you spend online every day, then what you need to do is reevaluate the priorities in your life.

It's not enough to say, "I've cleaned off my desktop and emptied my email, so now I'm organized and have more time."

You also need to create a "manifesto" for your digital life that defines the scope of how it will be used on a day-to-day basis. As the digital world becomes increasingly pervasive, this manifesto will help you stay committed to your important values and top priorities.

Think of it this way: If you add up the time spent on *each* digital device, *every* day, then you probably have a closer relationship with the virtual world than you have with your spouse, children, or friends.

You know there's something wrong with this balance, and yet you still find yourself flipping open the lid or gazing at your iPhone whenever you have a moment to spare—or even when you don't.

Is this really how you want to live your life?

Our bet is that you want more than what your digital devices can offer, and this desire for more, can motivate you to define exactly how you want to spend your time.

To start, we suggest answering three simple questions:

- What do you really value?
- How do you want to spend your time and energy?
- What are your life priorities and goals?

Don't just gloss over these questions. Instead, **spend the next 15 minutes thinking about what matters in your life**. Odds are, most of your answers won't relate to the digital world.

Keep these responses in mind as you go through the remainder of this book. Identifying your values will not only help with digital clutter, it will also provide a guideline for how you deal with these devices as you move forward.

As an example, Barrie finds this values exercise to be extremely useful when she works on her business, and when coaching clients who are trying to find their life passions or make other big life changes.

If you're still stuck, then here is a great list of 400 value words[15] to help you answer these questions. Review the words and select five to ten top values for your personal and professional life. As you look at these values, define how they can be used in your life.

For example, if one of your core values is "dependability," how do you want to be dependable? You might say, "I want to be dependable by being available to my family when they need me, by producing projects on time at work, and by honoring my commitments to others."

Try this process with every value word you identify. Under each word, write down several sentences specifying how you want to practice the value in your daily life. As you work through this exercise, you will see how a busy digital life often undermines your values by consuming too much time and mental energy. Make notes about this for now, because we'll return to these values later in the book to ensure your "digital manifesto" matches these all-important values.

After you finish this core values exercise, consider your top life priorities. These are the areas (outside of sleeping and eating) where you want to spend the most time. They might include

[15] http://liveboldandbloom.com/05/values/list-of-values

- Work
- Time with spouse/partner
- Time with children
- Time with other family members
- Time with friends
- Exercise
- Health
- Hobbies
- Spiritual or religious activities
- Entertainment/recreation
- Tending to chores, housekeeping, projects
- Volunteering/community time
- Managing finances
- Personal development/learning

Consider an average week, and think about how much time *you want to* spend on priorities on a weekly basis. Then compare how much time *you actually* dedicate to them.

How does your time spent in the digital world interfere with these priorities? Does computer or smartphone time force you to forgo some of the "expendable" time with family and friends in order to focus on essential work projects or daily tasks? Is that what you want?

We'll admit it's often easier to spend free time surfing the Net or playing games on our phone rather than having an intimate conversation with our spouse or reading a book to our child. Plus, it's tempting to bring our work home and skip the evening workout routine.

The point we want to make here is that *awareness* is the first key to change, so be real with yourself about how you aren't supporting your life priorities.

You may also have important goals you want to achieve. Maybe you want to run a marathon, write a book, or finish a huge project at work. By clarifying and committing to these goals—even if they seem far in the future—you're creating clear guidelines for where and how to spend your time. Reaching long-term goals requires focus and discipline—

things that are hard to maintain when you're distracted by social media and surfing the Net.

As you read through the rest of this book, keep your core values and life priorities handy. Use them as a guide to help you as you clear digital clutter, and as you come to decisions about how you want to live your digital life moving forward. When you're fully aware of who you are and what you want, it will be much easier to simplify your digital life and focus more time on what really matters to you.

With that in mind, let's talk about how digital decluttering can free up your mind to focus on the important things in life.

The Benefit of the Digital Decluttering Habit

Both Steve and Barrie have experienced the transformative experience of removing unnecessary items from their lives. Whether it's physical stuff in your home or a dependence on technology, you often need to remove things from your life in order to move forward.

This "less is more" philosophy extends to the online world as well. When you organize your digital life, you'll have less of a desire to create additional clutter with unnecessary files and apps. You will also gain a perspective on what's truly important and what can be eliminated from your life. And that's what we hope you'll get by **building the digital decluttering habit**.

As an example, a few months ago, a friend of Barrie's made the decision to drastically pare down her Facebook friend list—not just to clean it up, but to improve her mental well-being. She implemented her own digital declutter project by starting with the area that brought the most negativity into her life.

Here's part of what she wrote to her friend list before cutting back:

Dear Facebook Friends,

Over the next weeks I will be slicing and slashing my FB friend list down to, well, almost no one. I've come to a point where the cons of FB outweigh the pros. It's always been a time robber, and I really have not had too much of a problem with that. Living so far away from my native country, it's felt like a way to stay in touch and connected to parts of myself that are not here.

I've justified much of my own FB activity as a mechanism to share my creative work. But honestly, I have active FB pages where I can do that, and I'll actually start curating those pages much more now than I have in the past with the distraction of my private timeline. That feels right. Facebook is nothing if not a double-edged sword. It's made me laugh, cry, and happily reconnect with people I otherwise would have long lost touch with. It's made me wish I were someplace other than where I am, taking a toll on my ability to be present in the wonderful life I have.

Sometimes it takes a drastic decision like this to get the ball rolling. You recognize the impact your plugged-in preoccupation has on your life, and going cold turkey might be the best way to change. You may not be ready to implement the dramatic shift Barrie's friend made with Facebook, but you will find by starting a declutter project in just one small area of your digital world that you'll be motivated to reclaim more of your time and life.

Why Decluttering is a Keystone Habit

On his blog[16], Steve talked about the importance of keystone habits, which create multiple positive effects throughout your life. The right keystone habit has a snowball effect, where a single improvement has an unintended impact on other areas you didn't initially consider.

For instance, Steve considers a daily exercise routine to be one of his keystone habits because it increases his focus while writing, motivates him to maintain a balanced diet, and inspires his creative thinking. All of

---

[16] http://developgoodhabits.com/keystone-habit

these additional benefits happen simply because he forces himself to exercise 30 minutes each day.

Done correctly, digital declutter can become *your* keystone habit. When you make that commitment to minimize (or eliminate) certain aspects of technology, it will have a trickle down impact on every area of your life—from improving your productivity to building better interpersonal relationships.

Don't believe us?

Then take a few minutes to review the 14 advantages of living a decluttered digital life.

14 ADVANTAGES OF A DIGITAL DECLUTTERED LIFE

What most people don't realize is it's much easier to become a digital packrat than it is to live as a household hoarder.

When you live with clutter in your home, you have to step over (or around) items in order to get anywhere. It's in your face all the time, and *most* people get to the point after a few days where they have to clean up their messes. However, we can go for years without addressing the accumulated clutter on our digital devices.

Clutter on your computer and phone is hidden away for the most part—*until* you try to find something. You'd be surprised at how much your life improves as a result of organizing and streamlining your devices.

In this section, we cover 14 advantages of living a clutter-free digital life.

Advantage #1: It speeds up your computer, phone, or tablet

Although the average lifespan of most computers is about three to five years, you can prolong your system's life by clearing out unused items.

If you've installed loads of programs, stored endless files, and collected albums of photos, your devices will show signs of stress. But when you get rid of unnecessary files, you'll find that your devices run much faster and will have more disk space.

Advantage #2: It boosts your productivity

Without all of the distractions on your devices (and the time required to locate a specific file), you will be more productive with your daily tasks. The reason is simple—when every item is easily retrieved, you won't interrupt the "flow" that's important for concentration and creativity.

Advantage #3: It improves focus and concentration

A streamlined device forces you to focus on the task at hand. Just think of it this way—all of the icons, incoming emails, and assorted notifications are distracting. And it's very hard to stay fully concentrated when your attention is constantly diverted by push notifications or software alerts. This requires you to divide your attention, which is a proven killer of productivity.

To illustrate this point, let's talk about a recent study conducted at Stanford[17] that evaluated the performance levels of multi-taskers. The researchers found that people who focus on one task consistently outperform those who multi-task.

We feel that you're multi-tasking when you switch back and forth from a random notification to a current project. Your mind is not 100 percent focused on the core activity, so you don't end up doing your best work.

Advantage #4: It strengthens the security of your computer

A cluttered hard drive can often be a security hazard. This is particularly true of the rarely used software that you don't remember downloading. Maybe you installed a free game that you will never play again. Hackers could potentially use old software updates to gain access to your computer. By eliminating unused programs, you remove a potential backdoor to your computer.

---

[17] http://news.stanford.edu/news/2009/august24/multitask-research-study-082409.html

Advantage #5: It reduces stress and frustration

Clutter can negatively impact your peace of mind. Most of us naturally want to live in an organized environment, so when an area is disorganized, some parts of our minds feel agitated because each item represents a task we have yet to complete.

This agitation extends to your digital world as well. In fact, if your job involves lots of computer time, then the majority of your day is spent in the digital world. That means organizing these areas will have a calming effect on your state of mind and prevent the frustration that comes from being unable to find the exact program or file you need.

Advantage #6: It builds your confidence

When you clean up your digital life, you'll feel better about yourself because you've completed what was once a daunting project. You'll also gain more confidence as you increase your time, energy, and concentration. All of these benefits lead to more success in work and life, which can have a positive snowball effect on your personal development.

Advantage #7: It makes you more disciplined

The process of creating a digital decluttering routine requires some level of discipline—even though we make it really easy for you. As you practice this habit daily, your willpower becomes stronger and stronger.

More importantly, once your devices are organized, you will feel more disciplined about keeping them that way. You won't want to undermine your hard work and your newly decluttered devices.

Advantage #8: It gives you more emotional energy

Clutter of any kind drags you down. It causes low-level agitation and anxiety that zaps your energy and makes you distressed. As psychotherapist, former monk, and writer Thomas Moore reminds us, "Modern life is becoming so full that we need our own ways of going to the desert to be relieved of our plenty."

There's a feeling of freedom that comes with an organized space, and the feeling is present when you declutter your virtual world as well. This extra energy gives you more time to focus on things that really matter to you.

Advantage #9: It invites creativity

When you aren't tied to your devices or distracted by the unnecessary interruptions, you leave room for creative thinking and deep-level planning.

Creativity requires reflection, focus, and freedom in order to thrive. Also, when we don't rely on the immediate gratification of the Internet for our questions or challenges, we strengthen our creative muscle.

Advantage #10: It improves your relationships

You already know how an Internet obsession can harm your relationships. The more time you spend online, the less time you have for real-world interactions. Every email, phone app, saved article, or social media post is a temptation to spend "just a few more minutes" in virtual reality.

If your devices are disorganized, you're spending even more time disengaged from those you care about, as it takes you more time to find what you need.

Advantage #11: It helps you prioritize

While decluttering your digital devices, you'll make dozens of decisions along the way about what to keep and what to delete.

These small decisions ("Do I need to read this article?") often lead to bigger decisions ("Should I just stop bookmarking all of these articles in general?"). These choices will help you gain a better perspective on how to should spend your limited time.

Advantage #12: It saves you money

Any action that improves your focus *can* improve your ability to make more money. When you waste time, it's either because you're distracted or you can't quickly access the information you need. We all know that time is money. When you save time, you will be more productive, which might lead to a job promotion or additional revenue for your business.

On the other hand, when your computer runs slowly or gets a virus, you're forced to waste time fixing this issue instead of focusing on activities that add value to your life.

Advantage #13: It helps you discover lost stuff

You will be amazed at what you find while decluttering a digital device. Just think about the times when you've cleaned out old boxes in your attic or basement. Odds are you probably found long lost documents, cherished family photos, or a memorable souvenir.

The same thing happens with technology. If you've had a computer for years, then it probably contains important information, projects, and photos. At the *very* least, you might stumble across a reminder of a happy memory.

Advantage #14: It gives you a fresh start

It's refreshing to start something over with a clean fresh slate. As mentioned before, decluttering is a "keystone" habit that positively impacts the choices made in other areas of your life. When you remove numerous items, you free up space that can be devoted to new and exciting tasks.

Now, the question you might be asking is, "How do I know what's important and what can be eliminated?"

The answer to this is significant because you don't want to permanently erase an item that might be needed down the road. In the next section, we talk about six types of clutter, and how to separate the important from the not so important.

PART III

GETTING STARTED WITH DIGITAL
DECLUTTERING

6 TYPES OF DIGITAL CLUTTER

The first step for beginning a 10-minute digital declutter habit is to look at the various kinds of disorganization on your devices.

People don't generally hang on to digital clutter because they're hoarders. We generally have a reason for letting things get out of hand, even if it's just laziness or procrastination.

In the past, Barrie felt that sorting out her computer clutter was a waste of valuable time—time that could be spent on her "real" work. She found filing, deleting, and organizing her digital information too boring and tedious, so she just didn't do it.

Odds are, you probably think of digital decluttering as a tedious task, which is why you've avoided thinking about it until now. You've had a nagging feeling in the back of your mind about the digital mess, but doing something about it felt overwhelming.

Laziness, procrastination, or avoidance may not be your reasons for shirking your clutter cleanup duties, but *something* has been keeping you from addressing this issue. That's why it's important to understand the **six types of digital clutter** and identify *what* can be eliminated from your life.

#1. Wishful Thinking Clutter

These items are everything you've saved because you hope to get to them *someday*, which includes old emails, unread e-books, e-zines, blog posts, bookmarked Web pages and free downloads. The list of "wishful thinking" clutter grows longer and longer, making it even more overwhelming to go back and do anything about them.

We hang on to these things because we all have a desire to improve ourselves, and we capture a brilliant idea or bit of inspiration whenever we come across it.

Here's what habit expert Leo Babauta of Zen Habits[18] says about wishful thinking clutter:

"Self-improvement books or literature on our shelves we haven't read, tools for building or making something, exercise equipment or yoga clothes, gardening tools or baking apparatuses, a dusty old bike or running shoes . . . there are lots of objects we don't actually use but hope to someday. Holding on to them represents the possibility, sometime in the future, that we will be better. We will improve. We hope, and as long as we hold on to those objects, that hope is alive."

His advice?

"Live in the present, not in the future. Do things right now that make you happy, and don't keep objects as placeholders for some perfect future that will never come."

Wishful thinking items are as exactly as described—wishful thinking. They are put aside for a day when you magically have more free time. And if you're like most people, then you know that the last thing you want to do with those moments of free time is to read through dozens— even hundreds—of pieces of content.

#2. Homeless Clutter

This is digital clutter that can't find a home on your device. It clutters various places on your computer or smartphone because you can't figure out where it should go, so it sits in a "temporary" location until you find a home for it. This could include items like documents, screenshots, downloads, photos, and everything in between.

Homeless clutter *might be* valuable, important information, *or* it could be "wishful thinking" clutter that needs to be pared down. Either way, if you can't find an item when it's needed, it doesn't have much value. The truth is, these items require a decision to be made, so it's easy to ignore them for the time being.

---

[18] http://zenhabits.net/crutches/

#3. "What If?" Clutter

You've scanned and stored all of your receipts for the last five years, and you just can't let them go. *(What if I get audited one day?)*

You've saved projects from the job you left two years ago. *(What if I need this stuff one day? It could come in handy.)*

You've collected dozens of articles and can't bear to delete them. *(What if I need to go back to them and remind myself of an important concept?)*

We all suffer from the "what if" syndrome, worrying that an item might be needed after it is deleted. Sometimes the "what if" clutter comes from our belief that we *should* hang onto it, even if we're not quite sure why. *"It seems important. Other people are hanging onto theirs, so I should hang onto mine."*

Think about all of the "what if" digital clutter you've collected over the years and how much of it you've actually needed or used. More than likely, you won't regret removing the bulk of this digital clutter.

#4. Disposable Clutter

You might have once thought it was worth keeping, or maybe you just never got around to letting it go, but you have bucket loads of digital information that needs to be either archived or permanently deleted.

If it's useless, unnecessary or outdated, it needs to be eliminated. But for some reason, it just sits on your devices happily taking up space. This is often where procrastination or laziness sets in.

Who wants to spend hours going through old emails, documents, and photos and tossing them out? It's not the most exciting way to spend your time. So you let it grow until it builds up into a sizeable problem.

#5. It's-On-Sale Clutter

You get an email notifying you of the big sale at your favorite store. You're offered a free download by signing up to a newsletter. You have links to multiple coupon sites, or you've downloaded the latest and greatest free app.

All of this on-sale clutter sits on your computer or phone unused (or expired) because they get lost in the shuffle, forgotten, or you never had time to get to them.

We think that, by holding onto all of these offers, we'll save money or get real value at some point. But more often than not, these "deals" turn out to be drains unless you act on them immediately and then trash them.

#6. Sentimental Clutter

Items that have an emotional attachment are often the hardest to eliminate because they relate to a happy memory or we're afraid of offending someone if they are deleted.

Our computers are yet another repository for these emotionally charged items. Old emails from friends or romantic partners, successful projects we're proud of, photos from numerous adventures—all of these digital reminders make us feel closer to a specific person or fun experience.

But these items lose their meaning when they get lost in the wasteland of online clutter. It's hard to feel sentimental when you can't remember where the sentiment is located. Who has time to go through all of these reminders of the past anyway? It's just another temptation to spend time online rather than in the real world.

While going through your devices you will find that most items fit into one of these six categories. When decluttering, we suggest you look at the item and identify the category it belongs in.

Now, when it comes to answering important questions about your digital life, we also recommend being completely honest with yourself about the current state of your digital life. To help you do that, we recommend answering the 21 questions listed in the next section.

Do You Have a Decluttering Problem?
(21 Questions to Ask Yourself)

At this point, you might be wondering *how bad* your digital clutter problem is. As mentioned earlier, physical clutter is easily apparent—it's almost always in front of you. Every crowded drawer, cabinet, or closet is visual evidence of the amount of "stuff" you've accumulated.

On the other hand, digital clutter is more insidious. You can't see thousands of old emails or the useless documents stored on your device. You aren't confronted with the vastness of the problem the way you are when you walk in your home and trip over piles of physical stuff.

It's much easier to cover up your digital clutter by simply clicking away from it or covering it with another tab. But somewhere in the sub-files of your devices, a little voice is calling out, "Clean me, clean me." And that little voice is begging you to take control and get your digital house in order.

The best way to begin this project is to get a clear picture of your current situation. Simply answer the following 21 questions with "yes" or "no," then total your "yes" responses. That will give you a clear idea of your current digital situation.

1) Do you almost always need to use the "search" tool to find something you're looking for?
2) Is your list of bookmarks so long you feel too overwhelmed to get to any of them?
3) Are you hanging on to hundreds or thousands of old emails?

4) Do you have emails from over five years ago?

5) Do you have project files and unneeded documents from over five years ago?

6) Do you use more than one email account[19] because of all the storage you need?

7) Do you have many duplicates of photos, and is it difficult to find a photo you need?

8) Is your hard drive or phone storage 75 percent full or more?

9) Do you have multiple accounts for similar things, making it hard to find stuff?

10) Do you have many apps on your phone you never use?

11) Is your desktop cluttered with icons?

12) Do you have folders or bookmarks of stuff waiting to be read that you never have gotten around to reading?

13) Is your computer running slower or having problems as a result of all the data stored?

14) Have you had security breaches as a result of not decluttering?

15) Do you have more social media "friends" than you can possibly keep up with?

16) Do you have dozens of videos and audio you don't need on your phone and/or computer?

17) Is your operating system trash bin full?

18) Have you failed to change your passwords in the past few months?

19) Have you failed to clear your history and cookies in the past few months?

20) Do you feel anxious and agitated by the clutter on your phone or computer?

21) Do you avoid addressing your digital clutter because it feels too overwhelming?

---

[19] http://www.wikihow.com/Create-and-Send-Basic-Emails-With-Outlook-Express

How many times did you answer "yes" to these questions?

If it was 10 or more, then it's pretty clear you've become a bit of a digital packrat. Fortunately, you're not alone. Plenty of people have allowed their technology to get out of control.

Furthermore, it's not too hard to systematically organize all your digital devices. In fact, you can chunk down this massive project into a series of bite-sized, 10-minute daily actions. Do this every day for the next few weeks to completely organize every device in your life.

So, let's get to work . . .

8 STEPS TO THE 10-MINUTE DIGITAL DECLUTTER HABIT

Barrie and Steve talk a lot about habits in many of their books. If you want to make sure you follow through on your digital decluttering efforts, then the best way to make this happen is to build this routine into your daily life.

In this section, we review the same 8-step plan Steve and Barrie recommend for building any type of habit that they cover in their book, *10-Minute Declutter*. Even if you've read that book or understand the principles of habit creation, it's worth reviewing these steps again to make sure you're successful with your digital decluttering efforts.

Step #1: Focus on the Decluttering Habit

There is a concept called ego depletion[20], which is "a person's diminished capacity to regulate their thoughts, feelings, and actions."

Ego depletion impacts our ability to form new habits because our supply of willpower is spread out among all the areas of our lives. Because of this, it's important to work on only one habit at a time. That way, your store of willpower can be channeled into building that one habit, increasing the odds of success.

For the sake of this book, we ask that you completely focus on the 10-minute declutter habit and avoid adding anything new to your schedule.

---

[20] http://www.developgoodhabits.com/ego-depletion/

Step #2: Commit to Decluttering for 30 Days

Some people say it takes 21 days to build a habit, while others claim it takes up to 66 days. The truth is that the length of time really varies from person to person and habit to habit. Some habits are easy to build, while others require more effort. Our advice is to commit to decluttering for the next 30 days (or a month to keep it simple). However, you may find you complete your digital declutter project before the month is over. If so, use that time to declutter something else in your home or office for the remainder of the month.

Step #3: Anchor Decluttering to an Established Habit

Your decluttering efforts should not be based upon motivation, fads, or temporary desire. Instead, decluttering should be instilled in your life to the point it becomes automatic behavior.

The simplest way to do this is to incorporate the teachings of B.J. Fogg and his Tiny Habits[21] concept. Simply commit to a very small habit change and take baby steps as you build on it. An important aspect of his teaching is to "anchor" the new habit to something you already do on a daily basis.

- "After I wake up, I will open my computer, tablet, or phone and begin my 10-minute decluttering session."
- "After I put my kids to bed in the evening, I will spend 10 minutes decluttering."

You get the idea. Simply find a habit you already do consistently, and then anchor your new behavior to it.

Step #4: Pick a Time for Decluttering

The best time to declutter is the time that works best for you. Since your devices are portable (unless you have a desktop computer), you can pretty much pick any time that's convenient.

---

[21] http://tinyhabits.com/

That said, remember that your decluttering habit should be done *immediately after* the trigger because this will eventually solidify into an automatic response to the cue.

Sticking to this trigger is especially important, as you want to create momentum and enjoy the feeling of immediate success. Starting and stopping your clutter-busting commitment will leave you feeling frustrated, which interferes with your brain's ability to turn it into an automatic action.

Be sure your trigger is something that happens every day (if you want to work on decluttering seven days a week). If you want to skip weekends or declutter every other day, you can certainly do that, but it will take longer for the habit to form. If possible, work on decluttering every day for the first few weeks.

If you decide to work on your clutter before you leave for work, the trigger should be something like brushing your teeth, taking your shower, or making coffee.

Waking up early is, in itself, a difficult habit to establish. If you have to wake up earlier to add the decluttering habit to your new routine, consider picking a different time to declutter. If you don't have trouble waking up early, then the mornings might be a perfect time. Just be sure you set yourself up for success with this new habit by avoiding any pitfalls that might throw you off track.

If you work on your digital decluttering once you come home from work, choose a time (and trigger) when you are still energized and won't have many interruptions. This might be immediately after you walk in the door or right after dinner. If you're a night owl and get your second wind after 9:00, then you can declutter before going to bed.

Step #5: Take Baby Steps

As discussed in Tiny Habits[22], the best way to create a new routine is to make micro-commitments and focus on small wins. Motivation alone won't help you. The danger of relying on motivation is that you don't

---

[22] http://tinyhabits.com/

have a backup plan for those times when you're not in the mood to declutter. Instead, you need to turn the routine into automatic behavior.

So while your long-term goal is to declutter for 10 minutes at a time, you should start slow and focus on building the routine first. It's more important to stay consistent and not miss a day than it is to do the whole 10 minutes.

Examples include:

- Deleting five emails.
- Moving five photos from your phone to iCloud.

Yes, these activities seem overly simplistic—but that's the idea here. You want to commit to something so easy that it's impossible to miss a day. Then, when you have successfully created the habit, you can do the full decluttering routine for 10 minutes.

Step #6: Plan for Your Obstacles

Every new routine will have obstacles. When you know in advance what your obstacles are, you can take preventative action to overcome them.

Examples of common obstacles:

- Boredom with the routine
- Uncertainty of how to organize information
- Uncertainty of what to delete
- Feelings of overwhelm, anxiety, or guilt
- Not knowing where to start

If you anticipate these obstacles, you won't be blindsided by them.

The simplest solution is to use a concept called "If-Then Planning," where you create scripts to help you overcome these obstacles. Here are some examples:

- "If I'm having trouble completing a morning digital declutter routine, then I will commit to a new time and trigger."
- "If I find myself taking too long to decide on what to delete, then I will set a timer and delete as much as I can quickly before the timer runs out."

- "If I'm struggling to organize certain documents, then I will delay this project and move on to a different one."

See how each of these statements helps you overcome the specific challenges that you face? Our advice is to create similar statements for all the roadblocks that might arise with the digital decluttering habit.

Step #7: Create Accountability for Decluttering

Track your decluttering efforts and make public declarations about your new routine. According to the Hawthorne effect, you're more likely to follow through with a commitment when you're being observed by others. To stick with the digital decluttering habit, you should let others know about your commitment to this habit.

Post updates on social media accounts, use apps like Chains[23] and Coach.me[24] to track your progress, work with an accountability partner, or post regular updates to an online community related to the habit. Do whatever it takes to get reinforcement from others in support of your new routine.

Never underestimate the power of social approval. Simply knowing you will be held accountable for your habit keeps you focused and consistent.

Step #8: Reward Important Milestones

Digital decluttering doesn't have to be completely mind-numbing. Focus on building a reward system into the process so you can take time to celebrate the successful completion of your goals. The reward you pick is up to you, but it's important to celebrate those big moments along the way.

Keep in mind that a reward doesn't have to break the bank. You could check out a new movie, enjoy a night out with your significant other, or simply do something you love that doesn't cost a lot of money.

---

[23] https://chains.cc/

[24] http://Coach.me

We tend to underestimate the importance of having "fun" while building habits. Often, though, having a clear reward for regularly completing an action will help you to stick to the new routine.

Those are the eight steps for forming the digital decluttering habit. Simply follow the steps outlined and determine the best time to perform your habit, and you can easily add this routine to your day.

Now that you understand the basics of habit formation, let's talk about how to get started.

8 ACTIONS FOR STARTING YOUR FIRST DECLUTTERING PROJECT

In the *10-Minute Declutter* book, we showed readers how to go through every room in their home—cabinet-by-cabinet, drawer-by-drawer, closet-by-closet—breaking down the entire process into bite-sized, 10-minute chunks.

Because organizing your home involves moving physical stuff around, we had to be careful that our system didn't leave readers with a bigger mess on their hands once they began a 10-minute project. For example, if it takes 10 minutes to empty a pantry, then these items would create a mess until the next 10-minute project.

So our suggestion was to create a staging area where you store these small projects without creating a big, messy pile of stuff. We also made the recommendation to spend the last few minutes of the daily project tidying up any mess you created.

Because your clutter is contained on your devices, you won't need to worry about leaving a bigger mess as you organize your digital documents. You can simply set a timer for 10 minutes, work on a project for that amount of time, and then stop when the timer goes off.

That said, you might want to make notes that will remind you where you left off or what you had to do next.

So as you begin this process, we recommend the following action items:

Action #1: Review habit creation skills, then pick a starting date and time

Once you understand the skills of habit creation and you've established an anchor and accountability system, set a specific date and time when you'll start this project. Make sure this doesn't conflict with any other appointments or obligations. Remember, you're building a habit, so consistency is the most important consideration.

Action #2: Stick to 10 minutes

Start by digital decluttering for only a few minutes during the first week. This will make it easier to turn this project into a habit. After that, you can declutter for the whole 10 minutes.

While you might be tempted to do more, we recommend sticking to the 10-minute routine because it'll be easier to get started when you set an achievable goal. What you're doing here is avoiding feelings of burnout that often happen with a brand new habit.

Action #3: Find a quiet space free from distractions

If you're constantly being interrupted, you won't finish your decluttering project, which makes it impossible to build this habit. Before beginning the first project, find a quiet place in your home, office, or elsewhere to use consistently. Remember, this habit needs to immediately follow an anchor, so the location where you declutter should be near the place where you complete this established habit.

Action #4: Create the ambiance you want

Some people prefer a quiet environment when they work on a project. Others like music or background noise. Pick whatever works best for you, but make sure it's consistent because this will become another important trigger for the decluttering habit.

Action #5: Shut down extraneous tabs and turn off notifications

Any distractions should be turned off, closed, or shut down. Don't allow any temptations to pull you away for 10 minutes. It's amazing how much time you can lose down the rabbit hole of a "push notification" from a mobile app.

Action #6: Start with the low-hanging fruit

Where do you start a digital decluttering project? We suggest you tackle the biggest problem area—the device that bothers you the most. It doesn't really matter *where* you start, just as long as you start somewhere!

Action #7: Make quick decisions

You will encounter items that you don't know how to handle. *Should you keep it? Delete it? File it somewhere?*

Try to make decisions as quickly as possible. If it's an app or download that you can easily download again, then go ahead and delete it if you don't use it on a regular basis.

Action #8: Create a holding pen

If you are unsure about what to do with specific items, create a "holding pen" where you can store them. For instance, you could create a file on your computer titled "Maybe" and store every questionable item there until you can come back and make a final decision. (We'll talk more about this when we go over how to manage the folders on your computer.)

Now, since we're on the topic of making hard decisions, we should also talk about what to do when you can't make a firm decision on a specific item. Since files and programs don't take up physical space, it's tempting to hold on to them—even when they no longer serve a purpose.

That's why, in the next section, we provide seven questions to ask whenever you're unsure about the fate of a particular item.

7 QUESTIONS TO ASK WHILE DECLUTTERING

If you get stuck making a decision on a particular item, the following questions will help you with that choice. Remember, you only have 10 minutes every day, so it's important that you don't get bogged down with a specific item.

As you work through the decluttering project, you want to ask the following seven questions. If you find that you're saying "yes" most of the time, then perhaps you should get rid of the item:

1) Is this item something I rarely use?
2) Whenever I look at this item, does it mentally drain me?
3) Is the information outdated?
4) Am I holding on to it because it seems like it "might" be important, but I don't know why?
5) Have I finished using it and see no reason to use it again?
6) Am I spending too much time weighing the pros and cons?
7) Is it related to a project I no longer plan on pursuing?

Don't underestimate the power of these questions. If you need to, print them out and keep them close by while working through your digital items.

At this point, you have created a habit plan, picked a start date, cleared a workspace, and adopted a set of questions that will help you make quick decisions.

Now you're ready to tackle that first digital declutter project.

We'll start with an area that troubles many of us that live in this age of constant connectivity—decluttering your social media activities. You'll find that the suggestions are pretty straightforward, but actually *doing* them will take a significant amount of daily effort and the willpower to stick to the new rules you'll create for your life.

PART IV

DECLUTTERING YOUR SOCIAL
MEDIA ACTIVITIES

17 STRATEGIES TO MINIMIZE YOUR SOCIAL MEDIA ACTIVITIES

Be honest with yourself: How much time do you spend per day on social media? Maybe you're required to spend some amount of time on it as part of your job. But all of us get lured into the siren's call of Facebook, LinkedIn, Twitter, Snapchat, and the dozens of other social networking sites that steal our time and attention from the real world.

You may not be aware of the lost chunks of time you spend on social media. It draws you into a black hole of pictures, updates, and cat videos, and before you know it, hours have passed and nothing has been accomplished.

As an example, Barrie has gone on Facebook many times to post something for business, only to get lost in the stream of images and updates—completely forgetting *why* she went to the website in the first place.

So, the question is, "Why are we so attached to social media?"

Here are two considerations that shed some light on this question:

1. Social comparison

We make social comparisons to feel better about ourselves and our lives. We assess our popularity, worth, and success based on the feelings, experiences, and comments made through social media. Also, when we aren't sure about how to behave in a particular situation, we can turn to social media to see what others are doing or saying.

2. Fear of missing out (FOMO)

Status updates make us feel more involved and connected. Now that we can be so much more easily involved in the lives of others through social media, we feel like we're missing a party if we aren't constantly plugged in.

Aside from the time social media steals from our day, it can create anxiety as we feel compelled to engage in the latest social media rage. Facebook alone isn't enough. Many of us are plugged into multiple social networking sites, with an exponentially growing list of friends and followers to keep up with. Before you know it, you're bombarded with so many updates and messages that you feel like you're buried under an avalanche of information.

Social networking can easily become a cardboard substitute for the pleasures of real-life experiences and relationships. When you find yourself checking social media while sitting at a dinner table with family or friends, you know something has to change. When you're so busy *documenting* the moment that you don't *experience* it, it's time to reconsider how you integrate social media into your life.

Fortunately, we have a few suggestions (actually, 17 strategies in total) that help you *minimize* the amount of time you spend on social media, while *maximizing* the value that you receive from it.

#1. Get clear on your goals

Rather than unconsciously allowing social media a place in your life, make a conscious decision about how and why you want to use it.

If it's a necessary part of your job, make sure you're getting a solid return on your time investment. Be clear about which sites attract your potential customers or help promote your message.

In your personal life, ask yourself how much value social media brings to you and exactly how much time you want to devote to it each day. Write down that amount of time in a place where you can see it, and make a commitment to yourself to stick to it.

#2. Track your time

Once you've decided how much time you want to spend on social media, start tracking how much time you actually spend. You may be surprised to see that what felt like 15 minutes was actually an hour. There's nothing like a dose of reality to help you change your behavior!

One way to track social media is through a tool called Rescue Time[25], which runs in the background of your computer and gives you a detailed report (broken down by time spent and overall percentages) of the sites and applications that you frequently use.

#3. Focus on two or three social media sites

Rather than trying to stay connected everywhere on dozens of sites, pick the top two or three sites that you find the most useful or entertaining. There is no need to have two memberships on sites that do the same thing, like Digg *and* StumbleUpon or Pinterest *and* Instagram.

Shut down, log out, or unsubscribe from any extraneous social media so you aren't tempted to check them or respond to updates.

#4. Set a timer

If you've set a clear time limit to spend on social media, set a timer for that amount of time every time you log in. When the timer goes off, shut down and click away. Be diligent about this so you know exactly how much time you're spending on social media.

#5. Prioritize your important tasks

Many of us check social media first thing in the morning, and we use it as a way of procrastinating on the real work that needs to be completed. Rather than prioritizing social media, use it as a reward. Get your important tasks completed first and then reward yourself with a few minutes on Facebook or Pinterest. Just be sure to set your timer!

#6. Purge your "friends"

---

[25] https://www.rescuetime.com

Do you have social media followers and friends you don't even know? Are you getting updates from people that you really don't want to see?

Take 10 minutes a day for the next few days to cull your list down to those who share your interests or anyone you want to connect with. If you have a hard time un-friending someone, unsubscribe from them instead, so you're not constantly distracted in your newsfeed.

#7. Follow with care

Before you follow someone or accept a friend request blindly, make sure you really want to invest any time and energy into this person. Many social media sites, like Twitter, make recommendations of people with similar interests you might want to follow. Be discerning about who you allow into your social media world. Consider following anyone who shares your content or sends you a direct message. These people are already qualified, since you know they're interested in what you're doing.

#8. Engage with care

"Like," share, and comment on Facebook posts from people you prefer to regularly see updates from. This will trigger Facebook's algorithm to show only the posts you really want to see.

#9. Turn off chat

Disable the chat function on Facebook and any other sites that have it. Don't tempt yourself to get into online conversations when you don't have the time or it isn't productive.

#10. Make friends into acquaintances

There's a tool on Facebook that many people do not know about. When a "friend" is changed to an "acquaintance," their posts are pushed lower in the Facebook algorithm and have a far lower chance of showing up in your feed.

To do this, go to https://www.facebook.com/friends/organize.

You'll find a list of your friends here, and with a simple click you can lower their status to "acquaintance" without alerting them to this change. You might consider this option for those who *are* close family and friends but who post on Facebook so frequently that your timeline is crowded with updates that you might not enjoy.

#11. Revoke access to third party apps

There are lots of tools that integrate with Facebook and Twitter. These third party applications require your approval for them to access your profile. They continue to run in the background and often use pop-up notifications that can be distracting.

#12. Consider removing cell phone apps

If you want to cut back your time on social media or remove additional temptations, delete your social media apps on your cell phone. Limit your social networking to your desktop or tablet only, and use your phone for calls and texts.

#13. Make a "real people first" rule

Consider making a personal commitment to avoid social media when you are in the presence of friends and family. If your spouse or kids are around, no checking Facebook. If you're out to dinner with friends, no sneaking a peek at the Instagram that just popped in.

Be fully present with the real people in your life rather than distracted by your virtual friends.

#14. Use social media management tools

You don't have to create real-time posts on social sites all day. You can make your social media hours much more efficient and productive by using a tool like VerticalResponse[26] to pre-schedule and post directly

---

[26] http://www.verticalresponse.com/

from your account. Or try a tool that manages multiple social channels like or HootSuite[27], TweetDeck[28], or SproutSocial.[29].

#15. Curate your own content

Most social media management tools let you view all of your feeds at once, but you still have to scroll through each one to look at the content. A cool site and app called Flipboard[30] lets you feed in a list of keywords you're interested in and then compiles content based on your interests. You can easily share content as well with just one click.

#16. Try "If This, Then That"

If This Then That (IFTTT)[31] is a tool that can streamline your social media activities, and to some extent your online life. It's a site that connects two other services together using simple if/then statements.

You can create your own IFTTT recipes or use many that have been created by users in the past. IFTTT works with all sorts of social media and other services like Facebook (profiles, pages, and groups), Twitter, Instagram, LinkedIn, YouTube, and Pinterest.

As an example, here are a few of the more popular social media IFTTT tasks that may help you organize your social media:

- Send all your Tweets to a Google spreadsheet.
- Update your Twitter profile picture when you update your Facebook profile picture.
- Automatically Tweet your Facebook status updates.
- Post all pictures posted to Instagram on Twitter.
- Archive photos you are tagged in on Facebook to Dropbox.
- Archive all links you share on Facebook to a single file in Evernote.

---

[27] https://hootsuite.com/

[28] https://tweetdeck.twitter.com/

[29] http://sproutsocial.com/

[30] https://flipboard.com/

[31] https://ifttt.com/

- Archive all photos you "like" on Instagram to Dropbox.
- Have your iPhone pictures emailed to you as you take them.

As you can see, there are many clever uses for IFTTT. Sure, most of them won't be useful to you, but you can definitely find a few that might streamline time spent on social media.

#17. Consider a social media hiatus

Imagine a couple of days completely unplugged from social media. It might make you feel a little anxious at first, but once you shut it down for a weekend or even a day, you'll be surprised at how relaxed and liberated you feel.

Plan a weekend when you commit to completely disengaging from social media—no checking or posting. Announce to friends and family your plans to do this, both to warn them and for accountability. Decide on something fun, productive, or relaxing you want to do instead. You may find you want to unplug more often!

Now, while social media is a major time waster, it's not the only area where people struggle. In fact, many professionals often experience a daily struggle with staying on top of their email inboxes. That's why, in the next section, we go over eight simple steps to gain control of your email.

PART V

DECLUTTERING YOUR EMAIL INBOX

8 STEPS TO ORGANIZE YOUR EMAIL INBOX

Email often causes the most anxiety with people. What was once a convenient way of communicating has morphed into a massive time sink full of overwhelm and stress. The truth is, if you don't regularly organize your inbox, it can quickly get out of control.

The sad fact is that it's now common to see otherwise organized people with inboxes full of unanswered messages. Not only does this make it hard for them to separate the urgent from the not-so-urgent tasks, it also creates a significant level of stress in their lives.

Fortunately, it *is* possible to have a consistently organized inbox—if you're willing to put the work into doing it on a weekly basis.

Now, Steve has written an entire book about this process called *Daily Inbox Zero* [32] that can help you successfully tackle your email issue. But in this section, we provide eight "quick wins" you can use to gain control of your inbox.

Step #1: Schedule a time for tackling your inbox

Odds are, decluttering your inbox will require multiple 10-minute blocks of time. How long this will take depends on your current level of email. If it's just a handful of emails, then one day is more than sufficient. But if you are dealing with hundreds—or even thousands—of messages, then this might take over a week of dedicated effort.

As always, we suggest setting aside a specific time each day to deal with email. This time should be short enough that it is "hard" to finish

---

[32] http://www.developgoodhabits.com/digital-inbox-zero

processing the messages you receive on a daily basis, but not too constraining that you can't unbury your inbox from all the old messages.

Setting a specific time for dealing with emails also helps build a strong habit. When you go through email at a specific time, this creates triggers and makes it part of your routine, instead of a project that you will handle *"when you have the time"*—because we all know that time rarely comes.

Step #2: Move all old emails out of your inbox

Decluttering your inbox can seem daunting if you have to sort through thousands of emails. If you've allowed things to get out of control like this, then you have two options:

First you could declare "email bankruptcy," which is an extreme measure but is also the best way to get a fresh start with your inbox.

Simply send a message to your contacts that lets them know that you have deleted all your old emails. If they are waiting for a reply on a specific issue, then ask them to send it again because you don't have the original message. After that, simply delete all your old emails and make that commitment to keeping a decluttered inbox moving forward.

Honestly, this a nuclear option that should be carefully considered. If you feel like there is *no way* to get unburied from your inbox, then this might be the best option. That said, if you only have a few hundred messages, then it's not hard to organize these emails—just as long as you carve out time for this daily habit.

The second option is to block out time for decluttering your inbox. This time could be a little as 10 minutes or as much as 45 minutes, but no matter what you pick, there should be a level of consistency where you can complete this activity on a regular basis.

If you decide to go with the second option, then here's how to do it in the most efficient manner:

- Sort by sender and group similar messages together.
- Unsubscribe from all junk email services.
- Delete (or archive) the information-only messages.

- Filter any messages that require a 5-minute or longer response or completion of a task.
- Work through the backlog of older messages as you keep your inbox clear of new messages.
- Resolve to keep your inbox clean on a day-to-day basis in the future.

Don't worry if you're unsure about *how* to do some of these tasks—we'll walk you through everything in the next few steps.

Step #3: Unsubscribe from unwanted lists

First, you need to decrease the volume of inbound email. When you *receive* fewer emails, you will have *fewer decisions* to make on a daily basis.

The easiest way to stem the tide is to unsubscribe from any advertising or autoresponder messages you get in your inbox.

Now, it's extremely inefficient to open up every message and unsubscribe using the link at the bottom of every email. A simple solution is a service like Unroll.me[33], which allows you to make a decision about every list subscription. Within a few minutes you can remove your email address from every list—all at once.

With Unroll.me you can also make exceptions and keep the subscriptions for the email services you do want (like Steve and Barrie's lists, of course).

Step #4: Use the 4 Ds to process your messages

The "4 Ds" are a vital component to this process because they help you make quick and effective decisions. Whenever you open an email, you have one of four decisions: *Delete it, Defer it, Delegate it* or *Do it.*

Here is a breakdown of each potential decision:

Delete it. The message isn't important or it requires no response. The simplest action is to get rid of it. If you think it *might* be important, then you will put the message into an archive folder.

---

[33] https://unroll.me/

Defer it. If a message requires a task that takes 5 or more minutes to complete, then defer it and schedule a date and time when you will do it.

One of the main reasons people get bogged down is that they try to take action on emails that require you to complete a lengthy task. For emails like this, it makes sense to estimate the time required, write down the specific action into your calendar, respond back to the recipient with a date when they should expect it and then filter the email into your "Follow-Up" folder. You can use the items on your calendar to schedule the rest of your week.

Another option for deferring an item is to use the Boomerang extension[34], which creates reminders for specific tasks.

Delegate it. You may not be the best person to handle the task. If you have a team or subordinates, then delegate the task to the appropriate person. After that, create a reminder in your calendar to follow up and make sure it has been handled.

Do it. If it takes less than 5 minutes to respond to an email or complete the required task, then take care of it immediately.

Using the 4 Ds is the quickest way to get through an inbox without requiring too much of your time. When you use these four options on a regular basis, you'll find that it's not hard to get through dozens of messages in a half hour.

Step #5: File completed messages into specific folders

There's something to be said about those feelings of "overwhelm." If your inbox is filled with hundreds of messages—even if you've replied to them—you might feel anxious when you see all these emails. That's why we recommend you remove all emails from your inbox on a daily basis. The only items to keep here are unread messages.

It's important to minimize the number of folders in your inbox because this will help you find any email that you might need in the future. We recommend creating four types of folders:

---

[34] http://www.boomeranggmail.com/

- Archives (any email that contains information that might be needed)
- Automated (any email newsletter that relates to a strategy you'd like to pursue in the future)
- Follow-Up (any email relating to a specific action that needs to be completed)
- Send (if you use an assistant to process email, then have this person filter messages that require your final approval into this folder)

You don't have to use these four labels for your folders. This is the process that works for Steve, but you might want to do things differently. The important thing is to create a system for filtering messages and stick to it on a daily basis.

Step #6: Streamline your incoming messages

Many people get triple-digit emails on a daily basis. If this sounds familiar, then you might need a more proactive approach to weeding down these messages. Our suggestion is to create a stringent filter system that sorts your messages *before* they land in your inbox.

Filtering works differently for *each* type of email client. Since there are countless email providers (and versions of the software used), it would be challenging to provide a detailed walkthrough for each one.

The best way to learn how filtering works is to go to Google and enter "filter emails in" + the email client you use. So if you use Office 365, then you'd search for "*filter emails in Office 365.*" Simply go through the walkthrough to learn how to filter the messages that land in your inbox.

Now, the core idea behind filtering is to create "rules" for different messages, which sends them to a folder based on specific parameters. You can sort emails in a variety of ways:

- Send certain messages to predetermined folders (i.e., defer them).
- Tag emails based on the action required (i.e., do them).
- Automatically forward certain messages to a subordinate (i.e., delegate them).

- Delete or archive emails after you've replied to them (i.e., delete them).

To give a specific example, let's say that you're always receiving a message from Bob, who cc's the entire team. This message doesn't require your response. Instead, you receive this message because Bob likes to update the team on the status of a project. What you could do with Bob's messages is filter them to a folder called "Team Review" that you only read on a weekly basis.

You could create all sorts of rules like this with email filtering. Just look at the most common messages that you receive and look for ways to redirect them away from your inbox.

Step #7: Create canned responses

Chances are you often reply back with variations of the same email . . . over and over. Perhaps there are *dozens* of messages that require a similar response. Imagine how much time could be saved if you could click a button and automatically create a detailed response for one of these repetitive questions. This is what happens when you use "canned responses."

A canned response is a prewritten email that's stored in your email client. Whenever you get a question that's similar to this message, you simply click a button and the email will be automatically populated with the response. All you have to do is customize the response to the person and change a line or two, then you can send an email that fully answers the recipient's question.

Creating a canned response is similar to filtering because each email provider has its own process. If you want to find out how to create one, simply go to Google and look up "canned responses" + the name of your email provider.

Finally, the best way to use canned responses is to keep adding to this library whenever you get a common question. You'll find that doing this as a regular activity will quickly minimize time spent in your inbox.

Step #8: Move collaboration out of your inbox

Your inbox is not the place for collaborative messages between team members. Even when you send courtesy copies (cc) or blind courtesy copies (bcc), it's pretty hard to track a conversation when there are different people replying back to different messages. This often causes confusion and chaos when someone missed an important task that was buried under a collection of messages.

The solution to the collaboration issue is to move all team conversations out of the inbox and into a tool that's designed for this type of conversation.

Specifically, there are two types of tools that can help you do this.

First, calendars help you track upcoming milestones and deadlines. The two most popular tools for this are Google Calendar[35] and Outlook Calendar [36] . With these tools, you can set personal appointments, schedule milestones, and coordinate the dates with other team members. You can also create specific colors for each person or a special event.

The second recommended tool is project management software (like Basecamp or Slack) that is designed to handle ongoing conversations. The value of this tool is that it provides a central location for tasks, to-do lists, files, and all ongoing communication.

With project management software, you won't lose files or miss out on an important conversation. All team members create conversations in a central location that tracks the entire history of the project. So whenever you have a specific question, you can review the conversation thread to figure out what was worked on or what a team member said.

More importantly, your inbox won't be filled with emails that don't require your response. Every message is filtered through the software, and you can simply review this every day, adding your thoughts whenever it's needed.

---

[35] https://www.google.com/calendar/

[36] https://calendar.live.com/calendar/calendar.aspx

Well, now that your inbox is organized, you're ready to tackle the biggest project of them all—your computer.

This is the device that many people use throughout their workday and often during their personal time. As such, it's a common experience to fill up your computer with files and software that are no longer needed. In the next section, we detail a step-by-step strategy for decluttering this device, and how to make sure it runs at maximum capacity.

PART VI

DECLUTTERING YOUR COMPUTER

The Truth about the Clutter on Your Computer

The computer (i.e., desktop or laptop) is the device where people keep most of their digital clutter. We use this device for pretty much everything—entertainment, work projects, photo storage, and software downloads. So you can see how it's easy to let a computer get filled with lots of clutter. In a way, it can easily turn into the virtual equivalent of the junk drawer where you store every item that doesn't have a home.

Unfortunately, whereas it's easy to organize a drawer, decluttering a computer is a lengthy project that could require hours of effort. To *truly* organize this device, you have to think beyond a simple file management system. What's often required is to complete a series of micro-actions where you delete software programs, reorganize files, eliminate unimportant items, and generally organize everything into a minimalist structure.

All of the things described above are why we've broken the decluttering of your computer process into a series of steps. Our suggestion is to complete *each* step before moving on to the next. Furthermore, some of them might take longer than a single 10-minute block of time, so this means making one of two choices: 1. Declutter your computer slowly in blocks of time. 2. Dedicate a few hours (or even a whole day) to completing the entire project.

It doesn't matter what you pick—the important thing is to make sure you get everything done before moving on to the next step.

No matter what you do, it's important to tackle the area that is often the biggest reason why you might lose or misplace important documents—your file management system.

How to Create a Simple File System

A great file organization system helps you maintain a decluttered computer. The problem? When you get busy, it's tempting to save a file on your desktop (or in a random download folder) "for the time being." You might only do this a few times a week, but eventually your computer will become a disorganized mess.

Fortunately, it's not that hard to organize your files. In fact, we recommend a simple filing system that allows you to save new files, quickly find important documents, and know where to look whenever you're trying to locate an item but can't remember its name.

This filing method uses a hierarchical system for your documents, which looks like this:

1) One main folder that contains ALL your files and documents
2) Six to ten 2nd level folders—each representing a major area of your life
3) As many 3rd level folders as you need within each of the 2nd level folders
4) One "archive" 2nd level folder where you maintain old projects

Don't worry if this all sounds a bit confusing. We will break this system down into bite-sized, easy-to-complete steps.

Action #1: Create a Main Folder

When it comes to your files, J.R.R. Tolkien might have said it best: "One folder to rule them all, one folder to find them . . ."

Okay, maybe you're not a fantasy nerd like Steve, but the important lesson here is to organize *all* your documents into a central location that's easy to manage on a consistent basis.

By default, most computers automatically save certain files in different locations. Some go in the "Users" folder, word processing documents are often saved in the "My Documents" folder, and all your photos are sent to the "Windows >>Pictures" folder.

This can be frustrating because, whenever a file is needed, you have to look in multiple places to find it.

The solution is simple . . .

Instead of maintaining scattered folders in half a dozen locations, you should create a centralized main folder with clearly labeled sub-folders and *sub*-sub-folders.

What you *call* this main folder is up to you.

Steve simply calls his "Main Folder."

Clever, right?

Action #2: Create Six to Ten 2nd Level Folders

The organization of the sub-folders (what we call "2nd level folders") in your main folder is also up to you.

Get started by thinking about the major areas of your life. Do you keep a large database of photographs? Do you use the computer to store important paperwork and receipts? Is your digital time mostly used for entertainment purposes, where you play games, listen to music and watch videos? Or is it used for your job or business?

Take time to *really* think about the areas of your life that require a good organization system. In the next step, you will create six to ten sub-folders, so it's important to understand the documents that require their own folders, and what will be stored in these sub-folders.

For instance, let's say you own a small business. You probably have hundreds of documents like scanned receipts, yearly expense tracking, itemized deductions, and photocopies of tax returns from the past seven years. In this case, it would make sense to create a dedicated 2nd level folder called "Taxes."

On the other hand, let's say you work at a traditional nine-to-five job. Your tax records might only consist of the 1040 form that's submitted every year, or only five to seven documents. In this case, these documents would be saved in a 3rd folder that's part of 2nd level "Finance" folder, which has other 3rd level folders like your investments, monthly bills, and retirement account information.

See how this works?

If not, consider this: Steve stores tens of thousands of documents on his computer, but he only uses eight 2nd level folders to organize these items. Here is a breakdown of these items—including a brief description of what he keeps inside each of these sub-folders:

1) Archives: Includes old projects that are no longer active.
2) Business Management: Includes every process, project list, and report for his online business.
3) Develop Good Habits: Includes blog content, Kindle books, Slideshare decks, and everything related to his habit brand.
4) Education: Includes the login information and downloads for every online business program he has purchased.
5) Finances: Includes documents like taxes, investments, retirement spreadsheets, and home purchase information.
6) Personal: Includes photographs, memorabilia, and random personal items.
7) Self-Publishing Business: Includes podcast episodes, show notes, and documents related to his forthcoming video course.
8) Working: Includes all the files that are used on a daily basis.

As you can see, the 2nd level folders aren't that fancy. Simply think of the parts of your life that might require a series of sub-folders and then create a broad category name that makes it easy to identify the *types* of files that will be stored in each one.

Action #3: Create as many 3rd level folders as needed

You probably store a variety of items on your computer, so it's extremely important to maintain an organized hierarchy of sub-folders within each 2nd level folder. For the sake of simplicity, these are called 3rd level folders.

Now, we agree that it's extra work to create sub-folders within a 2nd level folder. The common impulse is to simply dump every item related to a topic within this folder. But turning your 2nd level folders into a disorganized mess completely defeats the purpose of creating an organized system for your files. The benefit of multiple 3rd level folders is that you know *exactly* where to look if you need to find a specific item.

In a way, it's like keeping a series of drawers in your office. You might throw every item related to your business into one of these areas, but there is no organization because you don't have a clear understanding of what's inside each drawer.

The best way to organize these 3rd level folders is to use labels that are easy to understand at a moment's glance.

Using a previous example, let's say you have a 2nd level folder called "Finances." The structure of the 3rd level files could look like this

- Finances >> Bills (Paid)
- Finances >> Bills (Unpaid)
- Finances >> Budgets
- Finances >> Investments
- Finances >> Receipts
- Finances >> Taxes

Again, the labels you use for the folders are up to you. What's important is to think about the areas of your life that require their own "buckets." Then simply take the time to store each document in the appropriate area.

If you're still unclear about how to organize a 3rd level folder, here is an example from Steve's habit book business. If you remember from before, he keeps all of his documents in a 2nd level folder titled "Develop

Good Habits," which is the name he uses for this particular business. Inside this sub-folder are the following 3rd level folders:

1) Advertisements
2) Audiobooks
3) Blog Posts
4) Email List
5) Instagram
6) Kindle Books
7) Print Books
8) SlideShare
9) Translations

Nine folders might seem hard to manage, but Steve actually likes this system because it helps him quickly find an item whenever he's in a rush. For instance, if he needs to send a Kindle book to a reader, he knows that the only place to look is in the 3rd level folder called "Kindle Books."

You might think that this file system is pretty obvious, but it's amazing how often people store documents in different areas on their computers and then wonder why it takes them 10 minutes to find a particular item.

Action #4: Store old projects and documents in an Archives folder

As you'll see in a later section, sometimes you'll want to keep certain files and folders for "just-in-case emergencies," but you know these documents aren't a part of your day-to-day activities. In this case, the best place to put them is in an "Archives" folder.

An Archives folder is simply that—a place where you store old information that *might be* important, but isn't currently applicable to your life.

For instance, just think about a project that you no longer work on. In the future, you might want to restart it, but for the time being it's not a priority. You would keep this project in the Archives folder because if it was stored as a 2nd level folder, it would be either a distraction or a reminder of a small failure on your part. In other words, you want it *out of sight and out of mind.*

Our suggestion is simple—if you have a 2nd level folder that is no longer an active project, then transfer it to the Archives folder.

Now that you understand the basics of this file system, let's go over six ground rules for making sure these files are consistently organized.

6 WAYS TO ORGANIZE YOUR FOLDERS AND FILES

At this point, you have six to ten 2nd level folders, with numerous 3rd level folders inside each one. The question you might have now is, "How do I organize all of these documents?"

Well, our recommendation is to keep things as simple as possible because this is the key to making sure that you build a long-term digital decluttering habit.

Here are six ways to make this happen:

#1. Use obvious naming conventions

Use file names that clearly describe the nature of the content. The mistake that people make is that they use a default name like "document 1" or something similar. This can quickly get confusing when you have more than a handful of items. It only takes a few seconds to give a document a name, so create something that accurately describes the content.

The important thing here is to maintain the same level of consistency that you would with a folder.

So, if a file includes a date, then you should use it for *all* files—even if you don't think a date will be important for an item. Not only will this create a streamlined system, it will also help you locate a specific file at a moment's glance.

For instance, consider the file names that are often saved on digital cameras. They usually look like this:

- IMG_8745.jpg
- IMG_8746.jpg
- IMG_8747.jpg
- IMG_8748.jpg
- IMG_8749.jpg

Unless you are willing to scroll through dozens of pictures, it's not that easy to locate the right image. In fact, IMG_8745.jpg tells you nothing about the file. All you know is that it's a picture and it was taken right before IMG_8746.jpg.

A more effective strategy is to add dates and descriptions to the important pictures in your life. Like

- 07_04_15_Beach_Vacation1
- 07_04_15_Beach_Vacation1
- 08_23_15_NYC_Trip1
- 08_23_15_NYC_Trip2
- 08_23_15_NYC_Trip3
- 10_24_15_Fall_Foliage1
- 10_24_15_Fall_Foliage2

It's not necessary to create a unique name for each file, but it's important to add a modifier that helps you identify what it is and when it was created.

Another important consideration is to create a new file name for each *version* of a document. This is important for the times when you collaborate with other people and have to make sure that the document you're working on is the most up-to-date version.

As an example, during the collaboration between Barrie and Steve for this book, they always added unique modifiers to signify the version of the file, which looked like this:

- 1st_draft_10_minute_digital
- 2nd_draft_10_minute_digital

- 3rd_draft_10_minute_digital
- 4th_draft_10_minute_digital

This naming convention is important because it allows everyone involved to immediately identify the version that needs to be worked on.

Finally, it doesn't matter what naming convention you choose. The important thing is to **stay consistent**.

Whether you decide to add dates, modifiers, or other descriptions, the goal here is to make a choice and stick with it. Not only will this help you find every file in the future, it also builds the habit where you clearly label every document that's stored on your computer.

#2. Use as many levels as you need

Don't worry about having *too many* folders. If you have a large number of files, then it's smarter to put them into specific folders instead of simply dumping them all into one central folder. We recommend you create a folder for any project that has *five or more* documents.

To show what this looks like, here are the paths for two recent documents that Steve used. One is for his taxes and the other is for his business:

1) Main Folder>> Finances >> Taxes >> 2015 Taxes >> 2015_Expenditures.xls
2) Main Folder >> Develop Good Habits >> Kindle Books >> 10 Minute Digital Declutter >> 4th_draft_10_minute_digital.doc

As you can see, these multiple folder levels allow Steve to quickly locate any item. He knows that if he needs to locate any item related to his 2015 Taxes, there is a specific folder for it inside the Taxes 3rd level folder, which is inside the Finances 2nd level folder.

#3. Keep application files separate from data files

Application files run the programs that allow you to create other files. These are things like Photoshop, Word, and iTunes. These files are not essential (to some extent). They can be reloaded or reinstalled if your computer is wiped.

On the other hand, what you *create* with these programs (i.e., your personal media) is unique and likely cannot be recreated. These are the files you would grab if your house is burning down. They consist of your memories, important papers, and work—all the things that matter and can never be replaced.

The benefit here is to separate the items that matter from files that can easily be replaced. This distinction becomes important when you back up your computer or store items in "the cloud."

#4. Create shortcuts to specific files

File conflicts often happen when an item is saved in one folder and then a different version is saved somewhere else. This can be frustrating because, when searching for a file, you're not completely certain which document file is the right version.

The question you might have is, "*Why* would you save a file in two different locations?"

Well, sometimes you might want to keep a folder of your most commonly used documents. If you open something every day, then it makes sense to keep it in a folder that's easy to access while also having a copy in the normal categorized folder.

For instance, Steve has a 2nd level folder called "Working" that includes the final versions of all his Kindle books in PDF and Word format. These are stored in this folder here because Steve constantly needs to find the original file, make quick updates, submit to different book platforms, and send to readers. But he *also* keeps a copy of these files in the "Kindle Books" 3rd level folder. The problem is that when he updates these files in the Working folder, this *could* create a conflict with the versions stored in the other folder.

One workaround for this issue is to create a **file shortcut** for each book (from the "Working" folder) that is then added to each of the "Kindle Book" folders.

A file shortcut allows you to find a file or resource located in a different directory or folder.

If you have any doubt about where to store a document, simply create a shortcut into the other folders. Shortcuts take up no space and can make it easy to find the right documents.

Not sure how to make a document or file shortcut? Here's how to do it on a Windows computer:

1) Right click on the file.
2) Click "copy."
3) Right click on the folder you want to be the destination for the shortcut.
4) Choose "Paste Shortcut."

The process is similar on a Mac:

1) Click on the Finder icon at the bottom left of the screen (the leftmost icon in the Dock).
2) Click on the Folder, File, or Application.
3) Select the Make Alias option.
4) Select Copy and then Paste it into the desired folder.

Sounds simple, right?

Trust us . . . this one small trick will save you a lot of headaches down the road when you are scratching your head, wondering which of the files is the most current version.

#5. Create a "Working" folder that acts as a temporary inbox

In addition to the Main Folder, you should consider creating a folder that acts as a temporary dumping ground for saving items that require immediate action. This can be called whatever you want—Working, Inbox, Temp, Scratch, etc. The point here is to have a place where you can quickly store an item without cluttering your desktop.

Yes, this advice runs counterintuitive to the idea of the "One Folder" principle, but we also recognize that there *will be* moments when you need to quickly download a file and don't have time to look for the right place to store it. In reality, we only recommend creating a Working folder if you can fully commit to checking and clearing it on a weekly basis.

#6. Organize files by their types

Sorting files by their "types" is the easiest way to group and find files. Sometimes you don't remember when an item was created (or even what you named it), but you know it was a certain type of file (like an Excel file or a PDF). By sorting a folder by file extensions, you can quickly scan items and find the specific item.

For instance, a sub-folder could be organized like this:

- PDF
- JPG
- XLS
- Doc
- Txt

Not only does this create a decent format, but you can also arrange everything into a format where it's easy to scan the different file types and find a specific item.

Okay, at this point, you have a well-organized group of files. While you might have thousands of files, they're stored in a single folder that's easy to use on a daily basis.

Now let's move on to the final step to fully declutter your computer.

7 Steps for Creating a Minimalist Computer

As we've discussed, it's easy to turn your computer into a virtual dumping ground for random files. Perhaps you worry about misplacing an item, so you keep it on a desktop for the time being. Do this enough times and your computer will be buried under an avalanche of digital clutter.

The solution to this is to create what's known as a "minimalist computer." Not only will you neatly organize every file, you will also reduce your options down to the few areas that are most important to your life.

For instance, here is a screenshot of Steve's computer that shows the four items he keeps on his desktop (this was taken around Halloween, which is why he has a jack-o-lantern as his background image):

1) Main Folder
2) The Firefox Web browser
3) Recycle Bin
4) Master Time Tracker

Each item is an important aspect of his daily life, so he only keeps these items on the desktop. Everything else is neatly stored in the appropriate folder.

Now, it's not too hard to create a minimalist computer. In fact, you can do so by following seven simple steps:

Step #1: Create four folders

It's not hard to delete any file or folder. Simply click on it, select the delete button, and *poof* . . . it's gone. Things get a little trickier when you have to transfer an item from your desktop to a specific folder. That's why we recommend creating four temporary folders on your desktop.

Think of these folders like a staging area in your home. These won't be permanently stored on your computer—instead, they're used as a holding pen for certain items while you make quick decisions about their ultimate fate. With that mind, we recommend using four labels that are similar to decluttering your home:

1) Archives
2) Eliminate
3) Maybe
4) Move

Here's a breakdown of each folder:

The Archives folder is a topic we have already covered. This is a digital storage area for files that might be important one day, but shouldn't be part of a 2nd level folder. Usually these are projects or software that are no longer needed or used.

The Eliminate folder is the virtual trashcan. You don't necessarily have to create a new folder, since most computers come with a Recycle Bin. But sometimes it's easier to create this temporary folder that you keep just in case you need to retrieve a deleted item.

The Maybe folder is where you store anything you haven't made a final decision about. An item could be archived, eliminated, or moved, but you might still be unsure about its final fate. During the initial pass through your computer, we recommend storing every questionable item in the Maybe folder. Then you can come back to it during a future 10-minute block and meticulously go through each item.

The Move folder is where you store anything that will be relocated to another sub-folder. We recommend storing items here because you'll find that many of the files have a similar destination, and it's easier to cut-and-paste files in groups instead of doing it one at a time.

Step #2: Sort your desktop by file type

Both PCs and Macs come with a function where you can sort by file type. We suggest you sort and organize these items by their type because it allows you to make quicker decisions about where to send them.

Step #3: Start with easy wins

Looking at a disorganized mess can be a daunting experience. When you see random files, software programs, and downloads, you might be unsure about where to start. Our suggestion is to begin with a series of easy wins.

Start with the files that you can make quick decisions about. These are the items that you know can either be eliminated or archived. It should only take you split second to make a choice, so you'll gain a lot of emotional momentum by chipping away at these items first.

Step #4: Move all the files

Once you have deleted and archived many of the files, start "dropping and dragging" them into one of the four folders. Put important items into the Move folder, send any questionable file into the Maybe folder, archive any unused file, and eliminate anything else that's no longer relevant.

Step #5: Clear out the Downloads folders

We've all done it—you download a file to your computer and can't figure out where it went. Odds are you probably sent it to a section on your computer called *My Documents* or *My Downloads*, which are virtual dumping grounds that are the default locations on most computers.

It's not hard to find this download area. Simply look on your main drive (usually this is C://) and you will see folders like My Documents, My Downloads, My Music, My Pictures, and My Videos.

We recommend repeating the previous steps for each of these download areas. Simply go inside each one and put each file into one of the four buckets (i.e., Archives, Eliminate, Maybe, or Move).

Step #6: Repeat with every sub-folder

This step might take days—even weeks—depending on how many files you have on your computer. Go to each folder that's on your computer and repeat the same process that you did with the desktop and download areas of your computer.

Step #7: Move everything out of the Maybe folder

Once you've gone through the entire computer, it's time to open up the Maybe folder and make some hard decisions. Each file represents a hard decision that needs to be made—should it stay or should it go?

Take a few seconds to carefully consider each item. Check the date when it was created. Is it something you've looked at in the past year? If not, then perhaps it's time to go. But, if there is *any* possibility that you might need a file sometime in the future then it's best to move it to the Archives folder.

At this point, you have a completely organized file structure on your desktop. Every file and icon has been sorted into its proper location.

So congratulations are now in order. You have tackled the *biggest obstacle* in decluttering and organizing your digital life.

That said, a computer is just one piece of the decluttering puzzle. In fact, you probably have many other digital devices that require your attention. Odds are your phone and tablet also have a decent amount of clutter. So that is what we'll cover in the next section.

PART VII

DECLUTTERING YOUR SMARTPHONE AND TABLET

Smartphones: The Positives and the Negatives

"There's an app for that!"

We all remember this catchphrase from the Apple commercials. In the eight years since the launch of the iPhone, app technology has grown in leaps and bounds. While computers are best organized by creating folders and files, your smartphone is organized through a series of files called "apps."

Now, just as it's important to minimize the number of files on your computer, it's equally important to eliminate the apps you no longer use. Odds are you only open a few dozen apps each month. By eliminating everything else, you will not only reduce the amount clutter on your smartphones, you will also increase your personal productivity.

More importantly, when your smartphone is decluttered, you'll be less inclined to use the apps that distract you from the areas of your life that truly matter.

Side Note: To avoid repeating ourselves, we're going to use the phrase "smartphone" to describe both phones *and* tablets. Since both rely heavily on app technology, all the principles described are relatively interchangeable. So if you're wondering how to declutter your tablet, simply follow the same instructions that we outline in the next few sections.

Smartphones have grown beyond a simple device for making calls. They've now morphed into a digital personal assistant that adds value to your life in countless ways. Smartphones can be used to take notes, track your walking steps, remind you of important appointments, count your calories, or even become your personal mobile university through podcasts and online courses.

On the other hand, your smartphone can be a catalyst for a life wasted in the digital world where time is spent on pointless activities like reading "listicle" articles, playing games, spending hours on social media, or snapping 1,001 selfie photos. Now, we're *not* against using entertainment for relaxation purposes, but this time should be balanced with activities that add value to your life.

In this section, we go over two strategies for using smartphones to improve your life. Specifically, we cover

1) How to minimize the amount of clutter on your phone.
2) Eight types of apps to organize and streamline your life.

So let's get started with the first strategy.

How to Declutter Your Smartphone (9 Action Steps)

Before you can turn a smartphone into a digital assistant, it's important to remove as many unnecessary items as possible. In this section, we'll go over the nine-step process to make this happen.

Action Item #1: Delete apps you don't use

Let's start with the most basic of actions. If you've had a smartphone for any length of time, then there are many apps you no longer use. As with physical clutter, we recommend using the "one-year rule" to eliminate any item that hasn't been used in the past twelve months. If you barely remember downloading an app—or even using it—then perhaps it's time to get rid of it!

Action Item #2: Clear out self-created content

You don't need to keep every item on your smartphone. Either upload it to the cloud or save it on your computer. That way, if you need to access the file sometime in the future, it can easily be accessed through one of your backups.

There are three benefits to clearing out your phone: 1. It clears up valuable space. 2. It will be quicker to sync and backup your device. 3. It will make your smartphone run much faster.

It's not hard to clear out your self-created data. In fact, the process can fit perfectly into a 10-minute habit. Here's how:

- Sync or backup your phone before beginning. Store the files in a physical device or in the cloud. (We'll go into specifics about the cloud in a future chapter.)
- Spend 10 minutes deleting photos you don't need. This will help to clean your photo gallery before it becomes unmanageable.
- Dedicate another 10-minute block for deleting unwanted videos.
- Go through the Notes app, Evernote, and any other list app to identify the files that are no longer needed. When in doubt, create an "Archives" folder in Evernote and add any unnecessary items to it. (Depending on the amount of files, this task might take multiple blocks of time to complete.)
- Finish by dragging similar apps together to create folders. Our suggestion is to group them together based on important areas of your life. For instance, finance apps, game apps, graphics apps, or productivity apps. The names of these groups are irrelevant. What matters is that they are put into a folder that makes sense to you.

It might take a week to complete this decluttering process, but once it's done you'll have a clean and well-managed smartphone instead of a giant collection of apps that no longer have any value to your life.

Action Item #3: Choose multipurpose apps

You should download—even spend money on—multipurpose apps that offer different types of functionalities. The benefit here is that you only have one place to check for a specific area of your life.

For instance, there are many apps that track habits. Some let you track multiple habits, others "reward" you for creating habit streaks, and still others rely on virtual communities where users can support one another. But all of these features can be found in an app like Coach.me. This means you can use a single app for this area of your life, instead of a few different ones.

Take a hard look at your apps. Do you have multiple photo editing or productivity apps? If so, then identify the app with the best features, use it exclusively, and ruthlessly eliminate the others.

Action Item #4: Turn off notifications

Notifications kill productivity.

We will say this until we're blue in the face because the constant dinging from your smartphone makes it impossible to focus on important tasks.

Just think of those times when you are in a "flow state" and get interrupted by a text message. Odds are, when you respond to the text message, it's hard to shift back to the original task with the same level of energy you had before the interruption.

Be sure to temporarily turn off all notifications when focusing on a priority task. In fact, you might want to permanently disable notifications from certain apps (like your email inbox).

Studies show that it takes up to 23 minutes to get back to a fully engaged state after a distraction. This means that you lose a significant amount of productivity for every little "ding." Multiply this a few times a day and you can see how it can have a very negative impact on your ability to get things done.

Action Item #5: Use airplane mode (even when not on an airplane)

Airplane mode disconnects you from the Internet. If you are working on something that doesn't require a data connection, then you should put your phone on airplane mode.

Not only will this avoid an interruption, it will also prevent you from surfing the Web or checking your email.

Another benefit of airplane mode is that it saves your smartphone battery. Since GPS and data roaming consume a lot of energy, enabling airplane mode helps your phone last longer over the course of the day while also improving its shelf life.

Action Item #6: Organize your music files

Music lovers often want their tunes wherever they go (like Steve's brother, who wants constant access to his collection of forty thousand songs). While total drive space is growing rapidly, it will be a long time before you can store an entire catalog of music within your smartphone. This means you need to organize any music in the most efficient manner possible.

There are three solutions to this issue:

1) Make playlists of music and cycle through them. You will only have a handful of playlists with your personal favorites (around three hundred to five hundred songs total). When you get tired of these songs, simply make more playlists, upload new songs, and change out the old music.

2) Use 3rd party music apps. Apps like Pandora[37] or Spotify[38] act like your favorite radio station and allow you to play a "type" of music or let you build a library of your favorite tunes. The downside is that you have to either listen to commercial breaks or pay a premium fee to enjoy uninterrupted music. The benefit of these apps is that you won't waste time loading up your smartphone with music that takes up a lot of disk space.

3) Store music in the cloud. There is a new option that's available through iTunes called iTunes Match[39], which allows you to access your entire library through the cloud. The obvious benefit here is that you don't have to store any music files on your phone. Instead, all the content is streamed directly to your device.

Music (as well as videos and photos) are major hogs of disk space. But, if you implement any of the three strategies just discussed, you can enjoy

---

[37] http://www.pandora.com/

[38] https://www.spotify.com

[39] http://www.apple.com/itunes/itunes-match/

your favorite music while making sure there is enough space for other important files.

Action Item #7: Delete or archive video files

If you think music takes up too much space, then consider your video files. Cute cat videos and Vine clips are entertaining, but they can also quickly eat into the storage capacity of your smartphone.

The only videos you should keep are the ones you plan to watch frequently—like the video of your daughter taking her first step. Everything else should be deleted, stored in the cloud, or transferred to your computer.

Action Item #8: Remove old podcast episodes

Both Steve and Barrie are voracious podcast listeners, but they also recognize that these episodes take up a lot of disk space. And, as you probably guessed, we recommend deleting these files on a regular basis.

There are two ways to do this.

First, you should enable certain default settings in your preferred podcast player, such as deleting each episode after it has been listened to and limiting the amount of episodes that can be saved in the queue.

Most podcasts now use streaming technology, so if you want to listen back to a favorite episode, you can always download it again.

Second, if you need to follow up on a strategy detailed in an episode, you could create an Evernote Notebook specifically for podcasts. Each Note could include the name of the podcast, the episode where the strategy is mentioned, and a timestamp of when the concept was mentioned.

Another strategy is to use a podcast streaming service like <u>Stitcher</u>. While this is marketed as the preferred podcast app for non-iPhone users, Stitcher actually provides a better interface than the iTunes app.

Simply subscribe to your favorite shows, streaming the episodes directly to your smartphone. When you're done, you won't need to delete the files. It's the perfect podcast player for anyone who hates digital clutter.

Action Item #9: Delete texts and call history

Generally speaking, previous phone calls or text messages don't take up a lot of disk space—so this final action is *completely optional.*

That said, from a decluttering standpoint, you should consider going through your call and text history and deleting anything that's not important. The benefit here is that by eliminating the unimportant, you can more easily find the conversations that are important or relate to a happy memory.

After completing these eight action items, your smartphone will contain only the important apps and files. Now, what we suggest next might seem *counterintuitive*: You should add a few apps to your phone. Let's talk about this process and why it's important for living a decluttered digital life.

8 QUALITY APPS TO ADD TO YOUR SMARTPHONE

Think back to our conversation about how smartphones can act as digital assistants. Instead of loading up your phone with pointless clutter, you can install apps that not only enhance your life, but also create an organizational system that prevents many of the problems that often cause digital clutter in the first place.

There are many apps that can have a positive impact on your life, but in this section we go over eight types you should install, *why* they are important, and a few specific examples that you should check out.

#1. Note-Taking Apps

One of the best benefits of having a smartphone is capturing ideas wherever you go. You never know when inspiration will strike or you'll simply think of something that needs to be immediately written down. With a note-taking app, you can collect every thought and review it at a later date.

While there are many great note-taking apps, one really stands out from the competition—Evernote[40].

There are many advantages to using Evernote:

- It automatically syncs with all your devices.
- It allows you to upload audio, video, text, or pictures as notes.
- The desktop version comes with a Web clipper that lets you copy sections of a website for future review.

---

[40] https://evernote.com/

- It can be used to create checklists for all your projects and multi-step tasks.

Evernote is the go-to app in this category, so if you're looking for a single place to store every valuable piece of information, then this is the app to use.

#2. List-Making Apps

While Evernote is also the 800-pound gorilla in the list-making app category, there are plenty of others that have an extra level of functionality:

- Any.do[41]
- Paperless[42]
- Todoist[43]
- Taasky[44]

The benefit of these apps is that they make it easy to start projects on the fly, create a series of action items, and then check off these items as they're completed.

#3. Calendar Apps

Keeping an up-t0-date calendar is an important aspect of productivity. When you have a complete understanding of your projects and obligations, it's easy to turn out the "noise" in the world and know how each request for your time fits into your long-term plans.

Here are a few calendar apps that we recommend:

- Agenda Calendar[45]
- Any.Do[46]

---

[41] http://www.any.do/

[42] http://www.developgoodhabits.com/digital-paperless

[43] https://en.todoist.com/

[44] http://www.taasky.com/

[45] http://www.developgoodhabits.com/digital-agenda

[46] http://www.any.do/

- Google Calendar[47]
- Quick Cal App[48]

Don't underestimate the importance of filtering every opportunity through a calendar. If you're a busy person, then your days are filled with appointments, meetings, and personal obligations. The benefit of keeping a central calendar on your phone is that you can filter every request for your time through the calendar and give people a clear "yes" or "no" response. This is the perfect way to make sure that you're focusing on high value activities.

#4. Collaboration Apps

As we mentioned in the section about decluttering your inbox, one of the best ways to eliminate a large number of emails is to take project-related messages out of your inbox and put them into a central place where everyone can collaborate. This can be accomplished by using one of these three apps:

- Basecamp[49]
- Flow[50]
- Slack[51]

A good collaboration app helps you track multiple projects and conversations within a single interface. As an example, when Barrie and Steve formed a partnership for a major project, they decided to use Slack instead of email. This choice was largely based on how Slack can be used to manage dozens of sub-projects and conversations about each component. If they picked email, then they would have risked having an important question get buried under an avalanche of unrelated messages.

---

[47] http://google.com/calendar

[48] http://quickcalapp.com/

[49] https://basecamp.com/

[50] https://www.getflow.com/apps/

[51] http://www.slack.com/

#5. Goal-Setting Apps

Another way it's easy to get overwhelmed is working on too many projects. The solution to this is to maintain a condensed list of active goals and store everything else in a "Someday" Notebook within Evernote that's reviewed each month. Then, since you only work on a few goals at a time, it becomes much easier to track them with apps like

- 42goals[52]
- Coach.me[53]
- Goalsontrack[54]

Each of these apps is designed to help you identify habits related to a goal and then make sure you stick to them. In our busy lives, it's easy to forget about the important tasks that need to be completed on a daily basis. The benefit of goal-specific apps is that they encourage accountability and create positive reminders to continue important habits.

#6. Password Apps

Security needs to be an important consideration when it comes to protecting your digital life. The good news is that there are many password management programs that work on both desktop and mobile platforms. Here are a few that we recommend:

- LastPass[55]
- 1U Password Manager[56]
- KeePass 2.28[57]

We won't go into lengthy detail about password apps here because we'll cover this topic thoroughly in the next section.

---

[52] http://www.42goals.com/

[53] https://www.coach.me/

[54] http://www.goalsontrack.com/

[55] https://lastpass.com/

[56] http://www.1uapps.com/

[57] http://keepass.info/download.html

#7. Syncing and Cloud-Based Apps

Most of the major brands offer cloud services to work with phones and tablets from the ground up. They seamlessly send and receive data and files from the cloud. The benefit here is that these apps automatically backup your information—without requiring any action on your end.

Here are a few syncing apps that we recommend:

- iCloud[58]
- Dropbox[59]
- Box[60]
- Google Drive[61]
- Amazon Cloud Drive[62]

The benefit of cloud-based apps is that often your phone won't have enough storage for your data. Just think about it: Where do all those selfies go? If you are not sending them to some sort of cloud-based service, then your phone will quickly overflow and become useless.

By storing your files in the cloud, you can confidently remove old photos and items, knowing they will be stored in a secure location.

#8. The "Find My Phone" App

This is an app that every mobile user should have. (To find it, simply type "find my phone" into the search directory of your mobile phone.)

As the name implies, this app helps you find a lost smartphone by remotely activating the GPS and showing its physical location.

For instance, if you think you left your phone at a friend's house, you can make the phone ring or buzz with a text message, which lets your friend know where to find the phone.

Finally, if your phone is stolen, you can remotely delete the drive so that none of your data is compromised.

---

[58] https://www.icloud.com/

[59] https://www.dropbox.com/

[60] https://www.box.com/

[61] https://www.google.com/drive/

[62] https://www.amazon.com/clouddrive/home

Now, once you have installed the apps we've just listed, you will have a smartphone that can help run your life. At this point, you will have a fully decluttered digital life. But there is one last item you should consider—how to protect the information you keep in the digital world. In the next section, we'll provide a series of strategies you can use to protect yourself.

PART VIII

PROTECTING YOUR DIGITAL LIFE

THE IMPORTANCE OF PROTECTING YOUR DIGITAL LIFE

It's a scary world out there.

Hackers can easily break into your computer, email, and social media accounts. No matter how careful you think you are, it's almost impossible to prevent a determined person from gaining access to your digital life.

That's why it's important to protect your digital life by backing up your devices on a weekly—or even a daily—basis. The benefit of creating backups is that you can quickly recover if you're ever a victim of a hacker, or if something catastrophic happens to one of your devices. Odds are you will never *need* these backups—but it's always nice to have them for those "just-in-case" scenarios.

You might be wondering:

"How does backing up my digital devices relate to decluttering?"

The simple answer is that it minimizes those anxious feelings when it comes to protecting your digital life. As we've discussed before, one of the main reasons for creating the decluttering habit is to reduce a feeling of overwhelm when it comes to technology. By having all your information stored in a secure location, you don't have to worry so much about losing it all.

Just think of it this way: There are so many things that could go wrong with your digital presence, including theft, floods, fire, ransomware, hardware failure, or simple user error. All of these scary situations could cause you to lose your files—forever.

In this section, we'll talk about how to safely protect your digital life, while making the process as pain-free and automatic as possible. So let's get started by talking about a concept called "The Rule of Three."

Use "The Rule of Three" for Your Digital Backups

L et's get started by clearly defining what it means to back up your devices. By default, many computers will prompt you to do a backup on a regular schedule. But let's be clear here—**this is not a real backup**.

If your computer is fried, stolen, dropped into water, or shot into space, then this backup is irrelevant because there is no way to access the lost data.

Put simply, **a good backup require lots of redundancies**. This means that every file should be stored in both the digital *and* physical world. That way, no matter what happens to your computer, the files will be stored in a safe location.

In order to create multiple redundancies, you should follow the well-known principle called the "rule of three" or "3-2-1 backups."

It works like this:

- Make **three** copies of anything you care about, such as family photos, tax records, or digital souvenirs. Basically, anything that is truly important to you should have three copies.
- Use **two** distinct formats for backups. This could include Dropbox[63] and your hard drive, *or* your hard drive and a DVD copy, *or* a CD and a memory stick. Any of these combinations will offer you a backup in both the digital and physical world.

---

[63] https://www.dropbox.com/

- **One** backup should be stored outside of your home (in the "cloud" or on Dropbox or in a safety deposit box). This is important because, if something happens to your house (like a fire), you will still have access to your important files.

At first glance, keeping three copies of everything may seem a bit paranoid. But as Murphy often reminds us, "Anything that can go wrong, will go wrong."

Imagine losing ten years of photos, work, and memories in an instant. That's what *could* happen if you fail to create redundancies with your digital files. By using the rule of three, you will have a contingency plan if disaster ever strikes.

Now, this concept is only one part of the process for keeping your files safe. In fact, we recommend implementing a six-step process to create backups on a regular schedule—without taking up too much of your precious time.

6 Simple Steps to Backing up Your Digital Life

The goal of any backup plan is to automate it as much as possible. This will be a challenge as it is yet *another* habit that you have to do on a daily basis. Even if the action only takes 5 minutes to complete, it could turn into an action that you dread doing.

That's why, in this section, we'll go over a six-step process that helps you backup your files and doesn't take too long to do every week.

Step #1: Choose a schedule for creating backups

When creating backups of your digital files, there are two important questions to ask yourself:

1) "How often do I create or add new files to my devices?"
2) "How valuable are the files that I create?"

Let's say all your work is spent in the online world and you're constantly creating new content on a computer (like Barrie and Steve, who write every day.) In that case, it would make sense to back up your files on a weekly—or even daily—basis.

On the other hand, if you rarely touch your digital device, then you only have to worry about doing it every month or so.

Since Steve and Barrie believe in the concept of building great habits, we suggest that most people should **stick to a weekly schedule for creating backups**. This timeframe is frequent enough where a complete loss in data is only a small annoyance instead of a major catastrophe. On the other hand, it's not so frequent that all your time is spent backing up your devices.

As with most habits, we recommend sticking to a specific schedule—like the same day and time each week. On a long enough timeline, this schedule will create an internal trigger where you'll remember to go through this process *without* being prompted by an external reminder (like a calendar alarm).

For instance, a backup could be scheduled for 4:00 p.m. on Friday, since this is near the end of the workweek, when you're wrapping things up. At first you might have to create a reminder to back up your devices, but eventually you'll remember to do so without being prompted.

Honestly, *when* you do a backup is irrelevant. What's important is to pick a day and stick with it.

Step #2: Use the "one folder" system for backing up files

In a previous section, we talked about the "one folder" system where you store every file in a main folder, broken down by a series of 2nd and 3rd level sub-folders. One of the main benefits of this system is that you can quickly add the main folder into a physical device—like an external hard drive, USB drive, or memory card. Really, all you have to do is copy the main folder into the device and wait for this process to complete.

Step #3: Use two physical backups

This is when you'll use the "rule of three," where you create two physical backups of all your files.

Now, there are many options when it comes to storing your files. Some of them might be a bit outdated, but you probably have old technology that is collecting dust in your drawer, so you can use them to create a sense of security for your digital life. For instance, you could use external hard drives, memory cards, burned CDs, burned DVDs, or SD Cards.

Once you've selected (or purchased) two physical backup devices, create a simple label for each one. As an example, Steve backs up his files to two external hard drives that are labeled "Backup 1" and "Backup 2." Clever, right?

Step #4: Keep one backup "offsite"

One of your physical backups should always be kept "offsite." This should be a location that you go to every few weeks. In other words, it shouldn't be a hassle to go there on a regular basis.

You might wonder, "Why do we recommend two physical backup devices instead of one?"

The simple answer is that by having two devices, you can continuously swap them out and avoid driving back and forth to the offsite location.

For instance, Steve keeps his backup at his parent's house, which he visits twice a month. When he goes there, he drops off Backup 1 and picks up Backup 2. Then, when he creates the next backup, he'll go back to his parents and swap Backup 2 for Backup 1. Sure, this means that sometimes his physical backups won't include the most current version of certain files, but it's a good enough measure in case something ever happens to his computer.

Your choice of an offsite backup is up to you. If your family lives close by (and you visit them regularly), then this is the perfect location. But if that isn't an option, then the device can be stored in a storage unit or a safe deposit box.

Step #5: Use a cloud-based backup program

You might feel that physically backing up your files and storing them offsite is a bit antiquated. If that's the case, you should consider using a cloud-based program that automatically stores your files in its virtual servers.

There are many options here. The following tools provide the best mix of security and affordability:

- Dropbox[64]

---

[64] https://www.dropbox.com/

- Carbonite[65]
- Box[66]
- Apple iCloud Drive[67]
- Google Drive[68]
- CrashPlan[69]

There really isn't a "right" tool for backing up your devices. What's important is to pick one and make sure it automates your backups, which we'll cover in the next step.

Side Note: Again, we want to emphasize an important consideration. While cloud-based backups are useful, never rely on these sites as your solo catastrophe plan. This decision will basically leave your data in someone else's hands. Use cloud-based backups whenever possible, but don't put your complete faith in this technology.

Step #6: Create automatic backups of your files

Most of the tools listed above automatically backup (or "sync") your files on their servers. This means you don't have to worry about creating online versions of your data. The entire process is handled in the background, *without* you doing a thing.

For instance, Steve uses Dropbox for his automatic backups because it performs this operation seamlessly throughout the day. He doesn't have to schedule this activity. Instead, it just happens in the background while he works on other projects.

Now, when it comes to creating automatic backups, you should consider the following points:

- Read up on the costs of these services and what best fits your needs (some of these sites have "free" options with limited storage, while others charge on a monthly basis).

---

[65] http://www.carbonite.com/

[66] https://www.box.com/

[67] https://www.icloud.com/

[68] https://www.google.com/drive/

[69] http://www.code42.com/crashplan/

- Check out the "get started" links or documents to see how to use the service for your specific device.
- Be sure to use the "one folder" system that we mentioned before, because it's a lot easier to manually copy and paste folders between your devices.
- Remember that when you delete a file from your computer, the service will sync this deletion, so it will be gone forever. The lesson here is to make sure to create both a physical and digital backup of your important files.

As you can see, it's not hard to create a digital backup for your important files. In fact, most programs do it automatically, so you won't have to schedule this activity.

Now, we recognize that you might be apprehensive about storing your personal files with a cloud-based storage company. Perhaps you watch the news and have heard the stories about hackers who gain access to popular websites—even government agencies.

Perhaps you are wondering, "How secure are these sites?"

That's why, in the next section, we go over four major concerns about cloud-based storage and what it's like to rely on another company to protect your valuable information.

4 Concerns about Cloud-Based Backups

While we've recommended a few cloud-based backup companies, we haven't taken the time to fully explain this technology. Maybe you're a little scared about the idea of storing your personal information in a place that *could* be hacked. That's why we want to go over four major concerns that many people have, and remove any apprehension you might have about this technology.

Concern #1: "If the cloud-based service is hacked, my information is vulnerable."

This is absolutely true, and is a *very* serious concern.

While the big players in cloud storage take their security seriously (and have lots of safeguards in place), no system in the world is 100 percent secure from a dedicated team of hackers.

On the other hand, you should be aware that *right now* your personal information can easily be discovered by many sites that you probably already use. If you have an account on Hotmail, Gmail, Facebook, Microsoft, Flickr, or Google Documents, then you should know that your information is already stored on their servers, which makes this information vulnerable.

How does this concern affect you?

It means you should never store anything that is personally or professionally dangerous, such as passwords, sensitive personal information, or any pictures that you don't want released to the world.

On the other hand, if your computer is comprised of vacation pictures or boring work documents, then it's probably okay to store these files in the cloud.

Concern #2: "A lack of Internet means I can't automatically back up my information."

This *is* a limitation. However, most places you travel these days have some sort of wireless or Wi-Fi connection. All you need is an Internet connection and you have access to cloud storage.

Yes, if you travel often, you won't be able to continuously sync your devices. If that sounds like you, then you might want to consider carrying a physical storage device with you at all times, just in case you can't automatically sync your information.

Concern #3: "If the cloud service is down, I won't have access to my backups."

The major players in the cloud storage arena have built a reputation for always being available. There is a reason that Amazon and Google are *rarely* "down"—having a constant connection is one of their major priorities.

While most cloud services can be 99.99 percent reliable, accidents *can* happen. There could be a fire in the data center or it could lose power due to an unforeseen catastrophe. But these are rare occurrences that shouldn't impact your decision to use cloud storage for your information.

Concern #4: "The government can see my information with a warrant."

Once again, this is true.

However, the government can't get a warrant without probable cause. So if you are the CEO of a website like Silk Road, embezzling from your employer, or cheating on your taxes, then keep this information off the cloud. But honestly, if you are doing these things on your computer, the government can get a warrant to search that as well.

We can offer an easy fix for this concern: Don't break the law!

Cloud-Based Backups: Yes or No?

Using a cloud-based backup service requires putting your faith in someone else, so it's a little scary to think of what could go wrong. Sure, you might have valid concerns about the safety of these sites, but it's important to remember that these services are *part* of a backup plan—not the only place where you archive important files.

Moreover, if you're concerned about potential hacks, then we recommend **not** storing six types of files in a cloud-based backup service:

1) Copies of birth certificates
2) Copies of passports
3) Social security numbers
4) Unencrypted list of usernames and passwords
5) Unencrypted bank account numbers/information
6) Sensitive documents or pictures

Well, that's it for our conversation about backing up your devices. Now let's move on to another important consideration when it comes to protecting your digital life—creating strong passwords.

THE IMPORTANCE OF CREATING SOLID PASSWORDS

Security is fast becoming a very important consideration when it comes to protecting your digital life. According to Naked Security[70], the average person uses over 150 websites that require a login and passwords. Due to requirements for each site, most people have nineteen different passwords that they need to remember. That is far too many passwords to keep track of, unless they are easy to remember (which by their nature leaves you vulnerable to hackers).

Now, we'll assume that you are an adult, so we won't waste your time by preaching to you about the importance of digital security. Suffice to say that it has now become extremely important to protect *everything* that's stored in the virtual world.

Unfortunately most people fail to properly secure their digital life. Their passwords are either too weak or based around easy-to-find information like pet names, favorite books, family member names, or birthdates.

Creating hard-to-break passwords is an important consideration because it's yet another way to minimize anxiety and create a sense of security for all your devices.

So in this section, we'll talk about passwords and how to make sure you create ones that repel any hackers who try to access your precious information. Let's begin with the one question that many people have.

---

[70] https://nakedsecurity.sophos.com/

What Makes a Good Password?

We now live in dangerous times when hackers use all sorts of tools to quickly break passwords. They can spend 10 minutes gathering information about you and your family, input this data into a computer, and then crack your password a few minutes later.

Don't feel like you are "important enough" to attract the attention of hackers? The truth is, millions of people have experienced some type of hack or cyber-attack. It doesn't matter *who* you are—at some point, somebody will try to gain access to your private information. That's why it's important to create a strong password.

Here a few rules to make sure your passwords are hard to break:

1) Don't use words in the dictionary.
2) Don't use information tied to you or your family in any way (maiden name, first pet, anniversary, etc.) in any part of the password.
3) Use a mix of uppercase and lowercase letters.
4) Use at least one digit.
5) Use at least one special character.
6) Use a minimum of ten characters in your password.

These six rules offer a minimum amount of protection, but we suggest taking one further step and using a mnemonic-based password.

Using Mnemonics to Remember Your Passwords

Simple mnemonics can help you craft a difficult password—as long as you can remember it. Mnemonics are simply a pattern of letters, ideas, or associations that assist in remembering something.

For instance, Steve once used (but has changed) a mnemonic password based on this phrase:

"Bob Marley sang the song 3 Little Birds!" spells out the acronym: BMsts3LB!

This was a simple nine-letter password that had all the requirements of a good password—uppercase letters, lowercase letters, a special character, and a digit.

The only reason he stopped using this mnemonic is because it wasn't long or secure enough, due to the increasing prevalence of hackers who can crack passwords under ten characters.

If you decide to go the route of mnemonics, think of the books, authors, and musicians that you like. Then create a mnemonic like the one above and you'll end up with a decent password that's easy to remember.

For instance, you could write something like:

"Stephen King wrote a book called *Mile 81!*"

This would generate a password like: SKwabcM81!

The only qualifier here is that if you have a particular band or book that everyone *knows* you love, then you shouldn't use a password based on it. Just pick a name you like—*but don't love*—to create a solid password.

Using Password Managers

Even obscure passwords like the ones described above won't protect you from an aggressive hacker. In truth, a good a hacker can eat an eight-character phrase for breakfast in a matter of minutes. A better solution is to use a password manager like the following:

- Dashlane[71]
- LastPass[72]
- KeePass[73]

Password managers have a number of excellent features. Not only do they encrypt and store your passwords, they also create unique logins for each device that makes it almost impossible to replicate on another computer. The biggest benefit to these tools is that they can sync with other devices, so you don't have to worry about forgetting a complex password if you need to access something from a mobile device.

---

[71] https://www.dashlane.com/

[72] https://lastpass.com/

[73] http://keepass.com/

"When Can I Reuse a Password?"

Now, there's one last point we want to make about password security. Chances are you have a large number of logins and passwords. For example, Steve recently tallied up all his login information and realized he has sixty-seven total passwords. The question *you* might have is—when is it safe to reuse a password?

To be honest, some passwords don't matter because they're attached to an account that doesn't store important data or personal information, so it's not a big deal if one of these accounts gets hacked. That said, it *can* be a big deal if someone gains access to an account where you have private information (like a password that's used on another site or your home address).

You should be very mindful of a few basic rules for password security (without getting buried beneath hundreds of different passwords).

- Only reuse passwords for accounts that don't matter (i.e., websites that don't require personal information).
- Use unique passwords for *every* account where security is important.
- Create strong passwords (using the six rules mentioned earlier).
- Change your passwords once a year.
- Consider using one of the password management systems we mentioned before.

If you follow these simple rules, you'll have a higher level of protection than the average person who uses the same phrase for all of their digital devices. If that sounds like you, then we highly recommend completing the steps we outlined in this section and changing the password for every site where you keep important personal information.

Well, that's the end of our discussion on protecting your digital life. Our time is almost at a close, but before we go, we would like to move away from the daily habit and talk about an important process that you should follow every quarter.

PART IX

MAINTAINING YOUR DIGITAL
DECLUTTER ACTION PLAN

THE QUARTERLY DIGITAL DECLUTTERING HABIT

As we near the end of this book, we want to give one last recommendation—you need to repeat the process of decluttering your digital life every quarter.

This book shows you how to break down the decluttering process into bite-sized, 10-minute habits. But eventually you'll finish the project and move on to something else. Odds are though, you will slip up from time to time, and some of your devices will become a little disorganized. That is why you should **set aside time every three months to repeat some aspects of the digital decluttering process**. This quarterly schedule is important because it will minimize the amount of time spent on this recurring process.

In this section, we go over a number of computer "spring cleaning" actions, plus we'll show you how to automate certain tasks so this process doesn't take too much of your time.

Action Item #1: Clear out the Downloads and Documents folders

As we've mentioned before, both the download and documents folders are notorious havens for random files. Even if you cleaned up these areas before, there will be times when you forget and accidentally download files to these areas. The end result is that you'll have a mixture of pictures, PDFs, software installs, or even funny cat videos.

Once again, to clear out these folders, simply sort by the type of file, and delete the software installs (and other unnecessary items). This will leave you with a collection of personal files, photos, or music that you might want to save. Simply repeat the process from the decluttering your computer section (i.e., Archives, Eliminate, Maybe, or Move).

Action Item #2: Find and eliminate duplicate files

Eliminating duplicate files is a judgment call. If you only have a few on your computer, then it's okay to keep them. However, if there are hundreds or even thousands of these files, then this can significantly impact your computer's performance.

The truth is that it is time consuming and difficult to find these files, but there is a manual approach that can save you a little bit of time.

In Mac, click *All My Files*, order the files by selecting the name from the drop-down icon, then scan for files that have the same name. Delete any items that are duplicates.

In PC, you can use the search function to find file types with the same extensions, then simply look for (and eliminate) files that have duplicate names.

Unfortunately, this method is less effective if you've saved the same file under different names. An alternative idea is to use a software program to hunt them down. The programs listed below might cost a few bucks, but most of them offer a trial version that you can use to eliminate most of the problem files:

- Winmerge[74]
- Doublekiller[75]
- Duplicate File Finder[76]
- Duplicate Images Finder[77]

All of the above programs automate the process of finding duplicate files. They search through multiple folders, sorting the results by *day*

---

[74] http://winmerge.org

[75] http://www.bigbangenterprises.de/en/doublekiller/

[76] http://download.cnet.com/Duplicate-File-Finder/3000-2248_4-10300084.html

[77] http://download.cnet.com/Visual-Similarity-Duplicate-Image-Finder/3000-2193_4-10422191.html

created, file size, file type, and other variables. Then you look over the results, make a final decision on what to keep, and delete everything else.

Action Item #3: Run an anti-virus program

When it comes to digital decluttering, any virus or malware will seriously slow down your computer, which goes directly against a philosophy of wanting your computer to be fast, neat, and organized. As part of your quarterly cleaning habit, you should run an anti-virus program to identify and eliminate any file that might be harming your computer. Here are a few options:

Some of the best anti-virus and security programs include

- McAfee[78]
- Norton[79]
- Kaspersky[80]
- Bit Defender[81]
- Trend Micro[82]
- Zone Alarm[83]
- Webroot[84]
- AVG[85]

Since each program has its own set of instructions, we encourage you to check out the above list, pick one based on your budget, and immediately install it on your computer.

---

[78] http://www.developgoodhabits.com/digital-mcafee

[79] http://www.developgoodhabits.com/digital-norton

[80] http://www.developgoodhabits.com/digital-kaspersky

[81] http://www.developgoodhabits.com/digital-bitdefender

[82] http://www.developgoodhabits.com/digital-trendmicro

[83] http://www.developgoodhabits.com/digital-zonealarm

[84] http://www.developgoodhabits.com/digital-webroot

[85] http://www.developgoodhabits.com/digital-avg

Action Item #4: Delete unnecessary programs and apps

The reason many computers are slow (or buggy) is because they are full of unnecessary software programs that require a lot of RAM to run. These are the programs that significantly increase boot up time and can also affect how quickly your computer operates on a day-to-day basis.

That's why it's important to get rid of those rarely (or never) used programs. Think of it this way—would you keep items around your home if you haven't used them in the past few years? The same rule applies here because this virtual junk is decreasing the long-term functionality of your computer.

Now, if you are hesitant about getting rid of a program, do a simple exercise: Create a new spreadsheet and keep track of the programs you use for the next three months. Anything not on this list should go during the next scheduled decluttering session.

Action Item #5: Clear your browser history

Your browser history is useful because it helps you quickly find the websites you use on a frequent basis. That said, when you have accumulated a large number of pages, they will take up space and even slow down the processing speed of your computer. That's why it's important to erase your browser history every three months *or* use a program to automatically do it on a set schedule.

To start, here are the manual ways to clear your browser's history on the different platforms:

- **Chrome:** Go to the "Gear" Icon >> Tools >> Clear Browser Data
- **Firefox:** Go to History >> Clear Recent History
- **IE 9:** Go to the "Gear" Icon >> Safety >> Clear Browsing History
- **Safari:** Choose History >> Clear History
- If you feel this is too tedious to do on a regular basis, then you can automate the process in the following ways:
- **Chrome and Safari:** Unfortunately, there isn't a way to automate the process unless you use a third party program.

- **Firefox:** Go to your Options >> Privacy, which shows the history of your browsing. Find the checkbox that says "Clear history when Firefox closes," tick this box, and it will automatically clear your browser history whenever you shut down the browser.
- **Internet Explorer 9:** Go to the *General* tab and tick the box for "Clear browser history on exit."

Clearing your browser history is a personal choice. While it does *slightly* slow down your ability to search the Internet, it's not much of noticeable difference. Some people like having a record of their searches, while others don't. If you like having the ability to find all the sites you've visited, then feel free to skip this step.

Action Item #6: Use a computer tune-up program

Chances are you have seen ads on TV for MyCleanPC (or others like it) that offer to thoroughly clear your computer of buggy programs. Unfortunately, most of these programs feed off fear or a lack of knowledge in customers. Their "free versions" remove nothing, or even worse might create "false-positives" on items that are important for the functionality of your computer.

Our point here?

When we talk about programs to tune up your computer, we are *not* talking about the programs advertised on television. Instead, we recommend free software that does a good job of cleaning up registry files, which can have a negative impact on the performance of your computer.

What are the characteristics of a good computer tune-up program?

Put simply, it should automate many of the tasks that you *could* do for yourself, such as

- Defragment your hard drive on a schedule
- Find and delete duplicate or unneeded files
- Uninstall files that never installed properly
- Check for driver updates that need to be downloaded and installed

- Control browser history (most will give options for periodic browser clearing)
- Choose what programs boot up when you turn on the computer
- Repair errors in system registry
- Delete temporary files

Sure, you can do all of this yourself, but using a software program will make the process a whole lot easier. The program that we recommend is CCleaner[86], which automatically cleans your computer by getting rid of those unwanted items and organizing those files you want to keep. It has a free version that works well, so you might not need to upgrade to the paid price.

In addition, there are a few other options you can choose from:

- Slimware Utilotoes: Slimcleaner[87]
- IoIo System Mechanic[88]
- AVG PC Tuneup[89]
- AShampoo[90]
- Comodo PC Tuneup[91]

From the "other" options, the best of the bunch may be IoIo System Mechanic, which has been rated as the best PC cleaning utility by *PC Magazine*. A fancy program like IoIo System Mechanic has a lot of little additions to help keep your computer clean and optimized.

Action Item #7: Clean your computer

Cleaning your computer sometimes actually means just that—physically *cleaning* your computer, which can include actions like removing loose debris and getting rid of dust that builds up in your fans.

---

[86] http://www.developgoodhabits.com/digital-ccleaner

[87] http://www.developgoodhabits.com/digital-slimcleaner

[88] http://www.developgoodhabits.com/digital-iolo

[89] http://www.developgoodhabits.com/digital-avg-pctuneup

[90] http://www.developgoodhabits.com/digital-ashampoo

[91] http://www.developgoodhabits.com/digital-comodo

The benefit here is that you remove the strain on the components and optimize the efficiency of your computer.

Fortunately, it's easy to clean your computer, so you can do it every quarter (or more frequently if you live in a dusty environment). Here's a simple process for cleaning your computer:

— **Step 1**: Turn off and unplug your computer.
— **Step 2**: Open up its side cases.
— **Step 3**: Use a compressed air can (or a soft bristled brush) to knock free any built-up dust.
— **Step 4**: Take a small vacuum cleaner and put it on the reverse setting to blow out the dust and debris from the chassis.
— **Step 5**: Put the vacuum on low power to suck out accumulated debris.
— **Step 6**: Replace the case, fully securing all nuts and bolts, then plug in and power up your computer.

Action Item #8: Repeat for your other devices

While your quarterly cleaning efforts will focus on your computer, it's equally important to repeat the same process for the rest of your digital life, including your smartphones, tablets, email inbox, and social media accounts.

Since each of these areas was previously covered, we won't waste your time by repeating ourselves. Suffice it to say, it's important to go back over the steps we listed for each area of your digital life, and make sure this is done every three months. Really, this is the one way to make sure that those small slips of disorganization don't snowball back into major issues.

Well, we're near the end of the book, so we'd like to end with a parting thought before you take action on the information that we've covered up to this point.

Conclusion: Get Started with Your Digital Manifesto

In the beginning of this book, we discussed the impact the digital age has on you, your relationships, and your lifestyle. We asked you to define your life priorities so you could have more clarity about where to focus your time and live your life.

Now we suggest you go back to those core values and review them once more. If you completed the values exercise we outlined, you defined specific ways you want to express your values through your choices and actions. And you looked at how your current life aligns with your chosen values and priorities.

It's always a little shocking to see how far our lives can drift from the values and priorities we hold dear, especially when we unconsciously hand over hours of our day to useless digital distractions. As valuable and efficient as computer technology has become, it has an insidious way of luring us away from our better selves and higher goals.

Now that you've completed the digital declutter process, you may see even more clearly how enmeshed your life has become with virtual reality. If you've made any headway at organizing and decluttering your devices, perhaps you've made a renewed commitment never to allow them to get so out of hand again.

In the last chapter, we offered you strategies for maintaining your digital declutter action plan and creating a quarterly review habit to keep things in order. But we'd like to suggest you go one step further . . .

We invite you to write your digital life manifesto. Now this may sound a little "woo-woo" or unnecessary, but without defining your personal principles in regards to your digital life going forward, it will be far too easy to slip back into old patterns and behaviors.

Allowing the digital world to slowly overrun your time and behaviors is far more serious than allowing your house to get untidy and disorganized. By checking out of the real world and losing yourself in technology, you're not only missing the fulfilling experiences and people around you, but also undermining your own mental and physical health.

The only way to prevent this disconnect from happening is by making a firm commitment to your intentions and actions, beginning today. And that's the purpose of your digital manifesto.

A manifesto is simply a written expression of that commitment. It serves as a reminder and compass in our lives, and guides our decisions. It is a safe place to return to in times of trouble when we may have forgotten who we are. Putting your intentions into writing has a powerful effect on your psyche. It's a way of sealing the deal with yourself and reinforcing your determination to follow through. In fact, it has more power if you write your manifesto in longhand rather than typing it.

You can write your manifesto as a paragraph, a personal contract with yourself, or simply bullet point reminders. The point is to put it into writing, share it with the important people in your life, and keep it in a place where you see it often.

To begin writing your digital manifesto, sit down with pen and paper, and answer these questions:

- How much time each workday is absolutely necessary for me to spend on my devices?
- Am I in a job that requires me to spend more time than I want behind my computer?
- How could I interact face-to-face with people in my work more often?
- How much time do I want to spend on my home computer doing work?

- How much time do I want to spend on social media for entertainment?
- How much time do I want to spend on my smartphone for entertainment?
- In what situations is a call or personal meeting more appropriate than a text?
- What real-life friendships have I neglected, and how do I want to nurture them?
- What family or relationship agreements should we have in place about using our smartphones, iPads, or laptops in each other's presence?
- What traditions or family time (like dinners together) do you want to make sacred and personal, without the presence of digital devices?
- What limitations or rules should we have for our children's use of digital devices?
- How should I be a role model to my children when it comes to these rules?
- When I have downtime, what are the top five best ways I should use it?
- How can I deal with the urges to "surf the Net" or engage in social media when I really don't want to?
- How often do I want to review this manifesto to remind myself of my values and priorities?
- How will I commit to managing my digital clutter so it doesn't get out of hand again?

At the very least, writing your digital manifesto will plant a seed in your mind about the boundaries you want to enforce related to your devices. You'll feel that little tug of guilt or discomfort when you log-on to Facebook when you're bored, or get hooked into a game that's lasting for hours. Just a little self-awareness can go a long way in helping you to break old habits and refocus your attention on more meaningful, joyful pursuits.

At the most, your manifesto can completely reorient your life and help you create stronger relationships and more meaningful experiences going forward.

The digital age isn't going away—in fact, it's getting more ubiquitous and distracting.

No one is going to step in and prevent you from falling down the rabbit hole of the virtual world. It's up to YOU to manage it for yourself, and that means taking preemptive action.

All of the information provided in this book isn't worth the paper or code it's written on unless you do something with it. We urge you to break free from bad digital habits, declutter your devices, and redefine the way you live your life.

Just a few minutes a day is all it takes!

We wish you all the best.

Barrie Davenport
www.LiveBoldAndBloom.com

Steve "S.J." Scott
www.DevelopGoodHabits.com

DID YOU LIKE 10-MINUTE DIGITAL DECLUTTER?

Before you go, we'd like to say "thank you" for purchasing our book.

You could have picked from dozens of books on habit development, but you took a chance and checked out this one.

So a big thanks for downloading this book and reading all the way to the end.

Now we'd like ask for a *small* favor. **Could you please take a minute or two and leave a review for this book on Amazon?**

This feedback will help us continue to write the kind of Kindle books that help you get results. And if you loved it, then please let us know.

MORE BOOKS BY BARRIE

...... *10-Minute Declutter: The Stress-Free Habit for Simplifying Your Home*

...... *201 Relationship Questions: The Couple's Guide to Building Trust and Emotional Intimacy*

...... *Self-Discovery Questions: 155 Breakthrough Questions to Accelerate Massive Action*

...... *Sticky Habits: 6 Simple Steps to Create Good Habits That Stick*

...... *Finely Tuned: How To Thrive As A Highly Sensitive Person or Empath*

...... *Peace of Mindfulness: Everyday Rituals to Conquer Anxiety and Claim Unlimited Inner Peace*

...... *Confidence Hacks: 99 Small Actions to Massively Boost Your Confidence*

...... *Building Confidence: Get Motivated, Overcome Social Fear, Be Assertive, and Empower Your Life for Success*

— *The 52-Week Life Passion Project: The Path to Uncover Your Life Passion*

All books can be found at: www.liveboldandbloom.com

MORE BOOKS BY STEVE

- *10-Minute Declutter: The Stress-Free Habit for Simplifying Your Home*

- *Crowdsource Your Success: How Accountability Helps You Stick to Goals*

- *Confident You: An Introvert's Guide to Success in Life and Business*

- *Exercise Every Day: 32 Tactics for Building the Exercise Habit (Even If You Hate Working Out)*

- *The Daily Entrepreneur: 33 Success Habits for Small Business Owners, Freelancers and Aspiring 9-to-5 Escape Artists*

- *Master Evernote: The Unofficial Guide to Organizing Your Life with Evernote (Plus 75 Ideas for Getting Started)*

- *Bad Habits No More: 25 Steps to Break ANY Bad Habit*

- *Habit Stacking: 97 Small Life Changes That Take 5 Minutes or Less*

- *To Do List Makeover: A Simple Guide to Getting the Important Things Done*

- *23 Anti-Procrastination Habits: How to Stop Being Lazy and Get Results in Your Life*

- *S.M.A.R.T. Goals Made Simple: 10 Steps to Master Your Personal and Career Goals*

- *115 Productivity Apps to Maximize Your Time: Apps for iPhone, iPad, Android, Kindle Fire and PC/iOS Desktop Computers*

- *Writing Habit Mastery: How to Write 2,000 Words a Day and Forever Cure Writer's Block*

- *Daily Inbox Zero: 9 Proven Steps to Eliminate Email Overload*

- *Wake Up Successful: How to Increase Your Energy & Achieve Any Goal with a Morning Routine*

- *10,000 Steps Blueprint: The Daily Walking Habit for Healthy Weight Loss and Lifelong Fitness*

- *70 Healthy Habits: How to Eat Better, Feel Great & Get More Energy*

- *Resolutions That Stick! How 12 Habits Can Transform Your New Year*

All books can be found at: www.developgoodhabits.com

ABOUT THE AUTHORS

S.J. Scott

In his books, S.J. Scott provides daily action plans for every area of your life: health, fitness, work and personal relationships. Unlike other personal development guides, his content focuses on taking action. So instead of reading over-hyped strategies that rarely work in the real-world, you'll get information that can be immediately implemented.

Barrie Davenport

Barrie is the founder of an award-winning personal development site, Live Bold and Bloom (liveboldandbloom.com). She is a certified personal coach and online course creator, helping people apply practical, evidence-based solutions and strategies to push past comfort zones and create happier, richer, more successful lives. She is also the author of a series of self-improvement books on positive habits, life passion, confidence building, mindfulness and simplicity.

As an entrepreneur, a mom of three and a homeowner, Barrie knows firsthand how valuable and life-changing it is to simplify, prioritize and organize your life and work in order to live your best life.

CPSIA information can be obtained at www.ICGtesting.com
Printed in the USA
LVOW10s2247010216

473248LV00005B/512/P

9 781519 555656